SACRED ART

The Resurrection

THROUGH THE EYES OF AN ARTIST

RON DICIANNI

SACRED ART

ISBN: 978-1-62050-142-9

Tapestry Productions 42065 Zevo Dr. Suite B4 Temecula, CA 92590 *www.TapestryProductions.com*

Ordering Information: Quantity sales. Special discounts are available on quantity purchases by corporations, associations, and others. For details, contact the publisher at the address above. Orders by U.S. trade bookstores and wholesalers. Please contact: Tapestry Productions Inc • 877.827.7763 *www.TapestryProductions.com*

Printed in Canada

Any painting can make you look, I hope mine can make you see...

–Ron DiCianni

THIS BOOK IS DEDICATED TO JESUS CHRIST,

Whose miraculous birth
Led to the most awesome life,
Suffering the worst death,
Resulting in the Resurrection that changed the course of history!

Because of You, death no longer scares me.

Acknowledgements

I must acknowledge those who have helped me with this book.

To:
My wife, Pat, who keeps encouraging me in the tough times. Honey, I love you.
My son, Grant, who not only came up with the title of this book, but the idea of how to go about it.
My son, Warren. What a grand model you were for this mural!
Finally, Mr. Byrd, the patron for the mural. Without his heart for the Resurrection to come alive to the masses, it would have never been painted. Thank you, my friend.

TABLE OF CONTENTS

INTRODUCTION 8-9

THE STORY 11-21

The Planning Process
Laying the Groundwork
Giving God the Best
Where to Paint
Setting the Stage
The Canvas
The Resurrection Story

THE CAST OF CHARACTERS 25

Abraham 27
Isaiah 31
David 35
Moses 39
Elijah 43
Noah 47
Esther 51
John the Baptist 55
Daniel 61
The Guards 65
The Angels 69
The Resurrected Jesus 73

EPILOGUE: THE MIRROR 80

A SPECIAL INVITATION FROM THE AUTHOR 87

ABOUT THE AUTHOR 89

INTRODUCTION

As the news cascades through the corridors of hell, demons rejoice.

"We did it! Jesus is ... dead!"

The party is short-lived as they begin to hear the footsteps of the Prince of Peace walking through the prison halls, opening up the prison cells and freeing the captives. Walking up to Satan himself, Jesus pulls the keys of hell and death from Satan, reducing him to a pitiful state in front of his hordes.

All of hell knows His story but hope it's not true. In the bowels of hell, they are now convinced — Jesus has triumphed.

In the world above them, the story unfolds just as God had planned. The man who claimed to be God in the flesh is killed by crucifixion. He is subsequently taken down from the cross and put in a tomb borrowed from a grieving friend.

The perpetrators of His death secure the opening to His tomb with a huge stone, which falls into a trench dug specifically to ensure closure. Its sheer weight would take a small army to roll it away.

Roman guards are posted at the tomb as "special forces" to guarantee that the body stays in and onlookers stay away.

Two days pass. As expected, death seems to have swallowed its prey, and the status quo is restored to the leaders of the day. Like the demons, they are now content to raise their hands in victory and congratulate each other for obliterating another contender for king.

Then the unbelievable happens. Sunday comes, angels descend, the Christ rises, guards faint, and the stone rolls away to reveal what everyone who hated Him hoped would not happen—the tomb is empty! What His killers now fear are headlines in the Roman newspapers. Suddenly, His terrifying words are remembered:

"Destroy this temple, and I will raise it again in three days" (John 2:19).

For the first time, it all makes sense to them, and nobody is laughing now — not His enemies, not the government, and certainly not the perpetrator of the plot. Satan's "aha" moment is now the realization that what he thought he achieved by killing Jesus was actually the very means by which heaven's doors opened to all. He can't conceive the irony. He failed spectacularly! He can do nothing but pound his fist on the gates of hell, which he now knows will soon be kicked down by the followers of the Victor — Jesus Christ, the Son of God.

In the pages of this book, you will have the chance to embrace the truth of what Satan would love to have you forget or ignore:

JESUS IS ALIVE!

THE STORY

Every artist longs for a definitive scene to paint, one that emerges from deep down inside their soul and becomes a masterwork that will influence the world for centuries to come. For Michelangelo, such a work was the *Creation of Adam*. For Rembrandt, it was *The Return of the Prodigal Son*. For me, it is *The Resurrection Mural*.

Some years ago I had a very successful show of my work at the Museum of Biblical Art in Dallas, Texas. More importantly, I became friends with the curators of the museum, and we stayed in touch. A few years later, I received news that the museum had a catastrophic fire. The facility was literally reduced to ground level; all the paintings were destroyed, including their "pilgrimage piece" (a work of art that was magnificent enough people would traditionally make a pilgrimage just to see). In the case of the museum, theirs was an incredible mural on Pentecost which had now been destroyed. After contacting the curators to offer my condolences and whatever help I might be able to give, I was told that they were unsure of ever even rebuilding.

Approximately two years went by before I received a call from the museum stating that they would indeed rebuild and they asked if I would consider replacing their pilgrimage piece with another mural. Much discussion followed, and I prayed. I was given only two demands: First, the work must be on the resurrection of Jesus. Secondly, it had to be sized at 12 feet high by 40 feet wide!

By God's grace, I had just finished four murals for the Assemblies of God in Springfield, Missouri. In years past I had rejected every mural request — even one from the Smithsonian. This mural suite had been my first foray into grand format painting and came out beyond my best expectations. But this mural of the Resurrection would be about five times bigger!

Now, as an avid student of those master artists who have come before me, I was aware that Norman Rockwell, possibly my most favorite painter, only attempted one mural of similar size. Apparently, he bit off more than he wanted to chew, because half way through Rockwell quit and another artist had to be called in to finish the mural. Armed with that knowledge, I needed to make sure God was calling me to this task. I felt like David against Goliath, but knowing how that story turned out, against all odds, I boldly gave the museum a "thumbs-up." My only hope was that God would give me the strength and power to do it. After all the "t"s were crossed and the "i"s dotted, I cleared my schedule for the next two years to devote myself to the mural.

The final result of two years of work? *The Resurrection Mural*, a 40 foot by 12 foot depiction of the Resurrection of Jesus Christ that hangs in the Biblical Museum of Art in Dallas, Texas and is the largest known contemporary Fine Art depiction of Christ's resurrection. Each day we receive calls and emails telling of how God has powerfully used this mural to proclaim His message of salvation through Christ to millions of viewers. But that's not where the story starts...

THE PLANNING PROCESS

Over the years I have been asked by countless people how a painting goes from blank raw canvas to a finished painting hanging in a museum or gallery. For me, the actual painting of a work is less stressful than hearing from God about what I am supposed to paint. I need to visualize the entire painting completed before I feel confident to dive headfirst into any painting, especially one of this magnitude.

Whenever I paint Scripture, I know I am on solid ground, but interpreting Scripture into a visual representation needs much prayer and a definite word from God. That was my first and most important task for the mural, so to my knees I went.

Two vital things emerged from that time of prayer. The first was that I knew that I did not want to repeat what other artists had painted in the past: an empty tomb, puzzled disciples, Mary Magdalene at the tomb, or Christ standing triumphant outside the tomb. None of these depictions stirred my soul, so I knew it was my task to come up with a new approach to grab the imagination of this generation. One scene that I had never seen an artist attempt was the Resurrection portrayed at the *moment* Christ came out of the tomb, in all of the blazing glory that could have exploded from the opening. I was sure that was what I was supposed to capture! Stopping that moment in time, with all of what is recorded in Scripture about it, became, for me, the way to approach this mural!

Secondly, I was led to Hebrews 12. The first verse reads:

"Therefore, since we are surrounded by such a great cloud of witnesses, let us throw off everything that hinders and the sin that so easily entangles, and let us run with perseverance the race marked out for us."

That verse hit me like a ton of bricks. Could it be possible that even at this moment, you and I are surrounded by some of these witnesses? If you could see into the spiritual realm right now, who would be surrounding you? Gideon? Jonah? Samson? Deborah? Jeremiah? If "a great cloud of witnesses" surrounds us today, I wondered how many would have been at the tomb at the very moment Jesus rose from the dead and took His first step out. I can't consider that even *one* of the great biblical characters would have missed that moment!

In the mural, my desire was to show which of those witnesses might have been close to the very opening of the tomb as Christ emerged. My only limitation was the size of the canvas. I tell people to imagine that the mural continues on for a hundred more feet in either direction to accommodate the many I could have included in the scene.

The actual tomb set constructed by Warner Bros.

LAYING THE GROUNDWORK

Most people don't understand what an artist goes through to accomplish a painting. I think there's a misconception that we hold out our thumbs (as portrayed in films about famous painters) and things magically appear on the canvas. Nothing could be further from the truth, especially for a painting the size of *The Resurrection Mural*! Let me be clear, artists don't "create" anything. Their value is in the skill to record things on a particular surface based on the reference materials from which they work. Which in this case made my job even more daunting, since I could not go back in time and see every nuance of what had happened when Christ stepped forth from the tomb. I would have to take great pains to "re-create" the scene with as much accuracy as was possible and trust God's leading for the details not recorded in Scripture.

My preparation for paintings, especially for one like this, can be compared to producing a small movie. I go through all the pains of production such as researching, casting, costuming, finding locations, prop making, and scheduling. Everything has to be worked out in advance, and if one thing goes wrong, it could cause a disastrous domino effect. Authenticity, excellence, and creativity are not things that appear by chance. I have to work hard at including those components, or find someone who can.

Before I commit to any artistic decisions on a work, I first sketch out "thumbnails" (small drawings which help work out composition and the overall direction of a painting). Once I have several of those completed, I

pour over the ones that have the possibility of becoming a larger work. Some are discarded immediately, others refined in further drafts. I then turn my thoughts to some very small, but practical, details that must be decided and ask myself countless questions. How many people should be in the painting? Who should they be? How are they dressed? What do they look like? Where do I get the costumes? What about the background? What exact time of day should it be? What are the environmental factors — sunlight, wind, etc? It would be dangerous to move forward before these questions and many others are answered. An analogy would be like starting a 1,000-mile road trip with a map or GPS for only the first five miles!

The starting point to any work of art is research. I try to find out how a particular character has traditionally been depicted. When we lack photographs of people who lived long ago, we have to defer to the material that the experts would most likely agree on. In addition it's important to consider any cultural associations with how those characters have been presented in the past — such as movies, plays, and the like. To go against the grain of what is commonly accepted would cause confusion for viewers and give them a reason to focus their attention on merely supportive parts of the painting rather than the central theme. For example, in *The Resurrection Mural*, if I did something very bright or odd with a character's clothing that caused one to look away from Christ, it could deter viewers from the entire vision of the message of the painting! Even though small things are important, when they become the focus of controversy, they could spell trouble for an entire work.

As you can imagine, none of the research is easy. Trips to many and varied libraries and institutions are needed before the information even begins to materialize. Most of the information is limited, and I have to put one piece in at a time, slowly letting it all come together naturally like a puzzle. The alternative is trying to force things into place, but over the years I have learned that such treatment only produces confusion.

GIVING GOD THE BEST

A major component in representing Scripture in visual form is that my effort has to be the best it can possibly be. For too long we have seen God get second best when it comes to the creative Arts. The Bible tells us in 1 Peter 4:10 *"Each one should use whatever gift he has received to serve others, faithfully administering God's grace in its various forms."* In other words, use your gift! But if it's not your gift, spare the world the agony! A gifted musician can soothe your soul; a non-gifted musician makes you want to pull the fire alarm! A gifted painter's work can make you see things that will affect you forever. A non-gifted painter's work will make you turn away.

I have been indelibly influenced by Malachi 1:8:

"When you bring blind animals for sacrifice, is that not wrong? When you sacrifice crippled or diseased animals, is that not wrong? Try offering them to your governor! Would he be pleased with you? Would he accept you"' says the LORD Almighty.

It is gut-wrenching and intolerable to think that the God of all creativity is often subjected to mediocre work from His children, only to find that they do better work for other "important" people. Who could possibly be more important

to us than God?

When I set about the making of the mural, I enlisted the best craftsmen I could find, sparing no cost. After all, God owns the "cattle on a thousand hills" (Psalms 50:10), and he also owns the hill. God can provide money! I was very blessed to have a patron for *The Resurrection Mural* who saw the need to spare no expense. I wish others who are blessed with riches would step forward and become patrons for the many great artists whose hands are silent because there are no funds to do what they are gifted to do. As I once heard said, "There is no lack of money in the Christian community. It's distribution that's the problem!" Amen to that.

Even the materials I used were the very best. My paints were imported from Holland. These paints are made in the same little place that provided paint for artists like Vermeer hundreds of years ago. One tube could cost up to several hundred dollars, and I had to buy 40 to 60 at one time!

When I researched the varnish to use on the painting, I conferred with the Getty Museum — and then went beyond their recommendations. When I talked with the company supplying the varnish, they suggested that I save money by going to a cheaper diluting material. I said no and purchased the best they had. It worked beautifully. Work done for God has to be the best we can do. If we are going to scrimp, let it not be on things that are for the King of kings. While I know that excellence in and of itself will never reveal God to anyone, the lack of excellence will definitely keep people from seeing God. When people reject the gospel, many times they are not rejecting the great news of the gospel as much as they are rejecting our bad presentation of it. God forbid that we should allow that to continue. Too much is at stake, including the reputation of the Almighty.

WHERE TO PAINT

For years my easel and studio have been a large part of my life. In Chicago, I had an entire addition custom built onto the house in which I could paint. But no house would accommodate a painting the size of a very large fire truck. So I went from my comfortable studio to a large, unheated, non-air-conditioned warehouse that had a 40-foot wall I could hang the canvas from. That was only half the battle. How to reach the top of the canvas? The answer was a 15-foot scissor lift like the one used on construction sites. Even my brushes had to be super sized. Some of my fine brushes I have had since Art school and the most delicate of those are little thicker then the tip of a pencil. It would take a long time with brushes like that! What I did not realize until I was suspended 15 feet in the air is that, first I'm deathly afraid of heights. Second, if it's 85 degrees at ground level, it's about 15 degrees warmer near the skylights. My summers were spent with sweat pouring down my face, my winters were spent using a hair dryer to thaw the paints and all the while I worried that if the scissor lift failed, I had no way to get down. But as always, God is faithful and He kept me through every moment!

SETTING THE STAGE

Years ago, before the camera, models were hired to pose for hours so artists could draw or paint them. Today's artists could never afford what it would cost to hire models to stand still for the months needed to complete a painting of that size! Thankfully, in today's digital age, we have cameras that show us the results of a photo shoot right on the spot. We can know in an instant whether we "got it" or not!

When it came to the monumental task of finding the perfect models for each character for the mural, I found new appreciation for what a casting director must go through. I painstakingly found each actor/model personally! Over the years, I have even been known to jump out of my car when I see the right model for a painting and desperately try to convince them right there on the street that I am not a crazy stalker but a bona fide artist with noble intentions. When you find what you are looking for, you have to act quickly or you will regret it forever. After all, many famous actors were discovered while simply going about their everyday activities.

For the actual photo shoot, I was fortunate to secure the services of an amazing Hollywood fashion photographer, Caesar Lima. Between his keen eye and great staff, we spent many days on set, photographing each model in a hundred different poses to ensure that every angle was covered. We ended up with about 1,200 digital images to choose from during the editing process! Quite a task! It was fortuitous that we did take so many, as plans and ideas often evolve during the initial production process.

When it came to wardrobe, I hired a professional designer with extraordinary skill and passion named Jennifer. We went through an exhaustive array of costume options for each character. Whether it was color or detail, the designer and I made all the decisions together. Nothing was left to chance, from initial concept to the final stitch. She designed and crafted almost every costume and also helped supervise the costuming when we were on location, making sure that each costume fit perfectly and all the folds fell as intended. The centurion costumes were borrowed from my good friends at Impact Productions. Additionally, Jennifer and I both hunted down every accessory that would adorn the costumes, from fasteners to necklaces to bracelets. I visited more antique stores in a month than most people do in an entire lifetime!

The life-size wings for the angels were made by the same prop company in Chicago that made Michael Jordan's wings for a Nike commercial! (I actually have another set of wings that I normally use, but the wings I wound up using, made of turkey feathers and a whole lot of wire, worked best.)

◄ An alternate posing we explored for the angels

A small scale exact model of the tomb built by hand

They attached to the models by a hidden vest with holders that allowed the wings to be rotated as needed. When lit, these wings were simply beautiful.

When the time came to build the set, I searched every imaginable place I could think of to secure photographs of the burial place of Jesus. Finally, I knew that I needed to get experts involved if I was going to get the right background in 3-D, so I hired the legendary film company Warner Bros. to make the tomb exactly to scale. I oversaw the entire process and worked with the best in the business. Every line of the tomb, every block of stone, and even the texture was matched as closely as humanly possible to the tomb that is recognized as Christ's tomb in Israel. The craftsmen who crafted the tomb set for me were the same craftsmen who worked on the *Indiana Jones* films. All of that collective knowledge went into *The Resurrection Mural* and I felt good about giving God the best I could obtain.

It took some work to figure out how to portray Mount Calvary, the place where Jesus was crucified (also known as Golgotha, the Place of the Skull). The mount still stands there in Israel. It is sealed off from the public, but it can still be photographed from a distance. Eventually, after researching the face in the rock, I sketched it in only to find that I had broken a rule of painting. You cannot put a face that large into a painting and not have it become like a bull's-eye. I needed to turn the face away to better suit the composition. I sculpted the rock myself out of a much larger rock and then painted it until it looked as exact as the actual mountain reference I was using.

THE CANVAS

Artists have used canvas for hundreds of years. However, when I went to look for the canvas for this mural, I got the shock of my life. Before I took the commission of the mural, I thoroughly researched all my contacts and costs for the project. The company I found for canvas said there would be no problem in getting exactly what I needed when I was ready. It took a few months to work out all the commission details with the museum, and when I went to order the canvas, the company no longer made it in the size I needed. No problem, I thought. I was sure that I could go to a hundred different manufacturers and secure it from someone else.

As it turned out, every canvas manufacturer in the world had stopped making it in the size I needed! (Yes, I said "world") I felt like I had entered the Twilight Zone! I got so desperate that I began calling sailboat manufacturers, asking if they could sell me the canvas they use on their giant sails. Unfortunately, that type of canvas would not work for what I needed. My son tried helping me secure a canvas and actually got to the point where he was faced with the prospect of a noted canvas manufacturer telling him that their cutting edge 21st century solution was a huge raw canvas with "a guy, a bucket of coating and a mop to apply it"! I couldn't believe it had come down to that.

Finally, after weeks and weeks of research, I went back to Warner Bros. to see if they could custom-make one for me. This time I was dealing with a different department than the one that crafted the tomb, and my reception wasn't as cordial as I had hoped. I wanted them to see what the mural would eventually look like, so I brought a sketch of it on a CD to them the day I visited. On that particular day, their computer staff was editing a very evil movie with hideous images. I was quite offended, to be honest. However, when they put my sketch in the computers, the image of Christ exploded onto the monitors and blew their other images away! I think they were in such a state of shock that they didn't want me around after that, so I was told they wouldn't do it. The light sure blasted the darkness away on that day!

In the end, God provided a great company called Universal Imaging (they do work for Universal Studios), and they had one roll, exactly the size I needed, left in their inventory. I immediately told them to put my name on it and mark it sold!

As incredible as the creation process was for this mural though, it's not ***really*** where the story of *The Resurrection Mural* begins...

THE RESURRECTION STORY

Before the beginnings of time itself, God knew that you and I would need a Savior. The day Adam and Eve sinned, God's plan of salvation began to unfold. Sin separated man from God and there was no way back into the Garden of Eden after Eve took that first bite. None of this caught God by surprise. Before time began He had already crafted a plan to reconcile man back to Himself. God's plan was a way of redemption for the entire human race that would ensure we could never again be separated from Him. The price of that plan was the life of His one and only Son, Jesus Christ.

That story of God's planned redemption is the thread that runs through the entire Bible, from Genesis to Revelation. God's foreordained plan to provide a crucified and resurrected Savior is a cornerstone of Scripture. Unfortunately, the Church has relegated the death and resurrection of Jesus to the two months of the year that we call the "Easter season".

From Scripture however we know that the Resurrection of Jesus Christ is core to the very backbone of Christianity. Paul went so far as to say that if the Resurrection had not taken place, our faith is in vain, or "futile" (1 Corinthians 15:17). If you'll notice in Matthew's Gospel, the Chief Priests who had plotted Jesus' death made no attempt to cover up His crucifixion — it was His resurrection that they had to lie about! Simply put, the miraculous nativity of Christ, the virgin birth, the miracles Jesus performed, and His agonizing death by crucifixion would not have completed God's plan of salvation without the Resurrection. Only through the Resurrection do we have the assurance that what God did in raising Christ from the dead is what He plans for all who accept Christ as Savior and Lord of their lives. The climax of every line of Scripture can be found in an empty tomb. That's where God did His best work!

The plan of that redemptive work is found throughout Scripture, not just in verses but also in the lives of such worthies as David, Abraham, Noah and Daniel — just to name a few. These served as "Christ-types" foreshadowing the way in which God would offer salvation to the world. Which is why I included those figures, as well as others, in the "witnesses" that are depicted in *The Resurrection Mural*... ■

THE CAST OF CHARACTERS

Because the Bible is full of great men and women who were specially picked to be a part of God's plan to redeem the world, I had a nearly unlimited supply of characters from which to choose. Who should be represented in the mural? This may have been one of my hardest decisions. Even now, when some look at the mural, they ask why I left out characters like Peter, Mary (the mother of Jesus), and Paul.

The answer is fairly obvious, I think. Look closely at the mural, and you will see that the characters I chose are in the supernatural realm. That's why they are "ghosted" in some parts. All had already departed this life. Peter and Mary, however, were still alive at the time of the Resurrection. Paul was not even a Christian yet!

One of my challenges when selecting which characters would represent the "cloud of witnesses" was trying to find women. Outside of Esther, a queen, and quite well covered in movies and literature, there are not many women whom I could have included who would have been instantly identified by viewers. Some have wondered why I didn't include Rahab. Quite candidly, Rahab wouldn't be recognizable by any outward means, and she was also a prostitute. I have no doubt that Christ's sacrifice covered her sin – and God mightily used her as the great-great-great-grandma of King David — but as an artist you have to be cognizant when depicting something would be more controversial than constructive with the viewers. Esther, however, provides a very beautiful and soft presence to what may otherwise have been a very male-heavy painting!

What was pivotal in the choosing of each person was that each was in some fashion a "Christ-type." Simply put, each person had some aspect of his or her life that clearly pointed others to Christ, which in the end provided me the best basis on which to choose from such a long list of contenders. ■

ABRAHAM

Throughout our lives, God asks us to do many things: some bring us joy and others bring hardship and pain. Sometimes our paths go straight over mountaintops, and other times they wind through dark valleys.

But no one, aside from God Himself, has ever been asked to do what God asked of Abraham—to kill his only son.

The story is found in Genesis 22, but actually began many years before. Abraham and his wife Sarah were given very great and wonderful promises regarding their future generations. God said to Abraham:

"I am God Almighty; walk before me and be blameless. I will confirm my covenant between me and you and will greatly increase your numbers. ... I will make you very fruitful; I will make nations of you, and kings will come from you."
Genesis 17:1–2, 6

Only one problem stood between Abraham, his wife Sarah and the fulfillment of those promises: they didn't have any children and were well past the age of bearing them.

Abraham reacted to these seemingly hollow promises in the same way that many of us react to something seemingly unbelievable: he laughed! The Bible tells us that:

Abraham fell facedown; he laughed and said to himself, "Will a son be born to a man a hundred years old? Will Sarah bear a child at the age of ninety?" Genesis 17:17.

Humanly, Abraham had every right to think a joke was being played and he was the punch line! The facts were clear, and they all pointed to God being wrong in His promise.

Even for us, it sometimes appears that God's promises don't make any sense or that He is simply mistaken. But the truth, as shown in the story of Abraham, is that God follows through with His promises, no matter what the odds look like. Perhaps the greatest rhetorical question ever asked is directed to Abraham: "Is anything too hard for the LORD?" (Genesis 18:14).

As God had promised, a year later Abraham and Sarah held their newborn son, Isaac, in their arms. God did not have to "eat" His words, but Abraham and Sarah did as they now saw God's promise unfold in this wriggling little bundle of joy.

After the child grew, God tested Abraham's faith once again. Here's the biblical account:

Some time later God tested Abraham. He said to him, "Abraham!" "Here I am" he replied. Then God said, "Take your son, your only son, Isaac, whom you love, and go to the region of Moriah. Sacrifice him there as a burnt offering on one of the mountains I will tell you about." Genesis 22:1–2

In asking this of Abraham, God already knew the plan He had in store. However, Abraham only knew that his precious son was slated to be offered up as a sacrifice. This son that was promised, waited for, and cherished was now going to be taken away by the same One who gave him to them. It didn't make any sense.

You may be wondering how Abraham's story relates to the story of the Resurrection. Those who know about God's amazing gift of salvation can't miss the correlation to Christ in this story of Abraham and Isaac. As Abraham obeys and takes that long walk with Isaac and two servants, he makes an enormous statement of faith in God and His ability to raise the dead. When Abraham and Isaac came near to the place of sacrifice, Abraham tells the servants, *"Stay here with the donkey while I and the boy go over there. We will worship and then we will come back to you"* Genesis 22:5. How would Abraham and Isaac both come back, when Abraham was supposed to kill his son? The answer is beyond human comprehension. Abraham believed that even if God allowed Isaac to be slain, God could, and would, raise him from the dead! That's great faith!

Many of you know how the story ends. God is not so cruel as to ask Abraham to do what only He could endure. He provided a ram just before the knife could plunge into Isaac, and He stopped Abraham from taking the life of his son.

"Stay here with the donkey while I and the boy go over there. We will worship and then we will come back to you"

GENESIS 22:5

When I put Abraham into the mural with raised staff in hand, I imagined a flashback entering his mind. As Abraham is watching Christ emerge victorious from the grave, he relives the moment that he was spared the agony of sacrificing Isaac, only to realize that God did not spare Himself that same agony but offered up His only Son to death and the grave. But unlike Isaac, Jesus had the power to walk out from His tomb, defeating death for the first and final time for us all. Is it even imaginable to consider Abraham's joy and gratitude? Worship was the least he could do!

One of my best friends, who also happens to be one of the best artists on the planet, Thomas Blackshear, traveled from Colorado to California to pose as Abraham for me. Because Thomas is a committed Christian, he brought a lot of expressive emotion to Abraham, just as I had hoped he would. He not only put himself in Abraham's shoes but he brought creative insight to the character as if he were painting Abraham himself. We went through a lot of options in the photography that day, and Thomas gave me a lot from which to choose, for which I will always be grateful. ■

"I AM GOD ALMIGHTY; WALK BEFORE ME AND BE BLAMELESS. I WILL CONFIRM MY COVENANT BETWEEN ME AND YOU AND WILL GREATLY INCREASE YOUR NUMBERS. ... I WILL MAKE YOU VERY FRUITFUL; I WILL MAKE NATIONS OF YOU, AND KINGS WILL COME FROM YOU."

GENESIS 17:1–2, 6

ISAIAH

Jesus is known by many names, including Healer, Deliverer, Son of God, Son of Man, Bread of Life, the Vine, and most importantly, Savior.

Seven hundred years before Jesus was born, a prophet named Isaiah was given special insight into some key names that Jesus would bear. In his book, Isaiah pours out words that must have been as the sweetest honey on his lips:

For to us a Child is born, to us a Son is given, and the government will be on His shoulders. And He will be called Wonderful Counselor, Mighty God, Everlasting Father, Prince of Peace. Isaiah 9:6

Isaiah further prophesied what impact Jesus' coming would have on the world:

Of the increase of His government and peace there will be no end. He will reign on David's throne and over His kingdom, establishing and upholding it with justice and righteousness from that time on and forever. The zeal of the LORD Almighty will accomplish this. Isaiah 9:7

Wow! What powerful and amazing words poured from his lips!

Isaiah also records the incredible awe that he experienced when he saw a vision of God, in all His glory. As Isaiah gets a glimpse into the supernatural realm, he is blown away and humbled by the majesty that surrounds God, so much so that he responds:

"Woe to me! I am ruined! For I am a man of unclean lips, and I live among a people of unclean lips, and my eyes have seen the King, the LORD Almighty." Isaiah 6:5

Trying to capture that humility on canvas was no easy task, to say the least.

When Jesus began His earthly ministry, He even used these words from Isaiah to introduce Himself:

"The Spirit of the Lord is on me,
because He has anointed me
to preach good news to the poor.
He has sent me to proclaim freedom for the prisoners
and recovery of sight for the blind,
to release the oppressed,
to proclaim the year of the Lord's favor." Luke 4:18–19

As I painted Isaiah worshipping at the moment Jesus stepped out from the tomb, I envisioned this great wordsmith for the first time wordless in worship. No words can express the wonder of what he sees. He can only put his hand over his heart and with every beat rejoice that he had the privilege of being the voice that God used so many centuries earlier to merely begin to describe Jesus. I wonder if Isaiah might wish for the chance to go back and add to his list of names one more — Resurrected Savior! In the presence of his Savior, Isaiah could now truly grasp his previous words: *"Then you will look and be radiant, your heart will throb and swell with joy"* Isaiah 60:5.

Most certainly, Isaiah experiences with his own eyes what every prophet wished for — the fulfillment of their faith, as the King of kings conquers the grave.

The person who modeled for Isaiah is the noted artist Michael Dudash, who also happens to be a dear friend and fellow believer. Like Thomas, Michael didn't just pose; he *artistically* posed, knowing what I would need to make Isaiah's passion and humility come to life. I'd like to say that I directed these models; but honestly, God did, for I received from them a lot more than I asked. ■

"The Spirit of the Lord is on me,
because He has anointed me
to preach good news to the poor.
He has sent me to proclaim freedom for
the prisoners
and recovery of sight for the blind,
to release the oppressed,
to proclaim the year of the Lord's favor."

LUKE 4:18–19

Do you recognize this character? He is my fellow artist Michael Dudash. Michael had a flare for the theatrical quality I was hoping to achieve for the prophet Isaiah — it's almost as if Isaiah's prophetic words were about to burst forth from his lips.

FOR TO US A CHILD IS BORN, TO US A SON IS GIVEN, AND THE GOVERNMENT WILL BE ON HIS SHOULDERS. AND HE WILL BE CALLED WONDERFUL COUNSELOR, MIGHTY GOD, EVERLASTING FATHER, PRINCE OF PEACE. OF THE INCREASE OF HIS GOVERNMENT AND PEACE THERE WILL BE NO END. HE WILL REIGN ON DAVID'S THRONE AND OVER HIS KINGDOM, ESTABLISHING AND UPHOLDING IT WITH JUSTICE AND RIGHTEOUSNESS FROM THAT TIME ON AND FOREVER. THE ZEAL OF THE LORD ALMIGHTY WILL ACCOMPLISH THIS.

ISAIAH 9:6-7

DAVID

Next in the line of witnesses is David who bears the title that I hope someday will be said of me — "a man after [God's] own heart" (1 Samuel 13:14).

Most of us know David as the shepherd boy who courageously fought a nine-foot-tall giant named Goliath. Even though just a boy, David had already slain a lion and a bear with God's strength. Recognizing God's power to deliver him from any enemy, David had the courage to face the giant when he overheard the taunts Goliath made to the army of Israel.

Armed with only five smooth stones and a sling, David defeated Goliath and became a national hero. But he didn't let his heart believe his "press," as the saying goes. His heart continued to be humble. King Saul could not tolerate David's fame, and he began to think of David as a potential usurper to his throne. Saul's evil heart concocted plans to kill David, but God spared David each time. Eventually, Saul's fear came true. David, a mere shepherd boy secretly anointed by Samuel years earlier as king in place of Saul, finally took the throne.

> *". . . the LORD has sought out a man after his own heart and appointed him ruler of his people . . ."*
>
> 1 SAMUEL 13:14

Throughout David's life, he sought to honor God and rule the kingdom of Israel with righteousness, but he was not perfect. He failed miserably many times. The most notorious failure was when he stood on a rooftop and lusted after a woman named Bathsheba, who was bathing within eyesight. David committed adultery with Bathsheba, got her pregnant, and then conspired to have her husband killed, thus becoming a murderer. David tried desperately to hide his sin, until a prophet named Nathan brought it out in the open. How, then, could God have considered him a man after His own heart? Humanly, it makes no sense. However, spiritually, God looks at the heart of a person. It was not the size of David's heart that impressed God, but the depth of his heart. If we could have peered into David's body with a spiritual X-ray, we would have seen a large capacity to love and serve God. That is still what God looks for today. God doesn't look for perfect people because, outside of Jesus, there are none.

Throughout David's life, he maintained that huge capacity to love God and others, even though he knew what it was like to be honored, served, hated, mistreated, and betrayed even by his own wife and son. David resided in palaces and in caves. He slept in the king's quarters and in the fields. More than once, he ran for his life, and was even forced to pretend he was out of his mind to keep from being killed. But David knew God's anointing was forever, and he served his God and his people until his death.

As I began to think of how to portray David in the mural, my first instinct was to show him as a king but with a twist. David is one of three royal figures in the mural that I show kneeling before Christ. These earthly "royals" recognized that their exalted human status is paltry when contrasted with the true royalty coming out of the cave tomb (Esther and Daniel are the other two).

David is also showing humility. Wearing blue, the royal color of Israel, trimmed in gold, he bows his head and holds out his crown to Jesus. All of us will someday get the chance, like David, to lay our crowns at the feet of Jesus in recognition that He deserves what we were temporarily entrusted with. Even kings know the right posture when confronted with Christ. How I wish that many who are now in leadership would be so wise as to bow their knees here, because they will later on, when they stand before God.

David, a prophetic writer, had once written, *"My God, my God, why have You forsaken me?"* Psalms 22:1. Sound familiar? Jesus cried out those words while on the cross, when His Father had to turn away because of all the sin Jesus willfully took on Himself. David even described this scene of Christ at the cross: *Dogs have surrounded me; a band of evil men has encircled me, they have pierced my hands and feet. I can count all my bones; people stare and gloat over me. They divide my garments among them and cast lots for my clothing.* Psalms 22:16–18

Kneeling at the tomb, David now sees with his own eyes the other half of the story — the risen Christ!

The world-famous artist Morgan Weistling consented to pose as David for me. Morgan has been a longtime friend and has a relationship with Christ. I guess he reminds me a bit of David, not only physically, but also in his heart for God. Morgan fell into posing for David so naturally that for a second or two we were transported back to biblical times; it felt as though we were watching David himself. Artistically, it might be the best pose in the painting for me. ■

THE LORD SAYS TO MY LORD: "SIT AT MY RIGHT HAND UNTIL I MAKE YOUR ENEMIES A FOOTSTOOL FOR YOUR FEET." THE LORD WILL EXTEND YOUR MIGHTY SCEPTER FROM ZION, SAYING, "RULE IN THE MIDST OF YOUR ENEMIES!" YOUR TROOPS WILL BE WILLING ON YOUR DAY OF BATTLE. ARRAYED IN HOLY SPLENDOR, YOUR YOUNG MEN WILL COME TO YOU LIKE DEW FROM THE MORNING'S WOMB. THE LORD HAS SWORN AND WILL NOT CHANGE HIS MIND: "YOU ARE A PRIEST FOREVER, IN THE ORDER OF MELCHIZEDEK."

PSALMS 110: 1–4

MOSES

I have long envied Moses. Both he and Abraham were called "friends" of God (Exodus 33:11; James 2:23), and God treated them as such. As an artist, my mind explodes at the possibilities of being a friend of God.

Throughout Moses' life, he knew God had called him for a special purpose. From his short ride down the Nile River into the arms of Pharaoh's daughter to watching God write the Ten Commandments with His own finger to the parting of the Red Sea, Moses intimately knew God. Moses knew that his Friend was mightier than Pharaoh, so he bravely stood before Pharaoh and demanded that he release the Israelites to go and worship God. And even though Pharaoh treated him harshly, Moses saw his task through to the end. Again, as with David, Moses was not a perfect man. He committed murder at a young age, which started him on a training course in the wilderness for 40 years. It has been said of Moses that he spent 40 years running from God, 40 years running back to God, and the last 40 years being used by God.

It's clear that God uses flawed people. I am reminded of that every morning when I look in the mirror, and Moses was no different. What was different about Moses was that he knew the voice of God, whether it was at the burning bush or when he was leading the vast company of Israelites. Not only did he hear the voice of God but he also obeyed the voice of God with humility. When he was first called by God to lead the children of Israel, Moses replied, *"Who am I, that I should go to Pharaoh and bring the Israelites out of Egypt?"* Exodus 3:11. I had a similar response when I was asked to do *The Resurrection Mural*. My first instinct was to go pull the covers over my head and hide! But Moses and I both decided to persevere, and I know I am glad I did.

Moses is credited with writing the first five books of the Old Testament called the Pentateuch in Christianity or the Torah in Judaism. God revealed things to Moses, including things that happened before Moses' lifetime, so he could record them in writing for us. What I love about those books, as well as what's in the entire Bible, is that we are told everything — the good, the not so good, and the downright ugly. God used Moses in spite of his flaws, and that is one of the best lessons all of us can learn from him!

When I painted Moses, I was intimidated. He looms so

large over the landscape of Christianity that I didn't think I could do him any justice in my wildest dreams. Should I paint him like Charlton Heston, as a robust, virile leader? Or should I portray him as that humble man of God I earlier described? In the final analysis, I chose the latter, so as not to give the impression that God only uses those who "look" like heroes. He uses those with hearts like heroes! Aren't you glad?

Moses stands erect with the tablets of stone, the Ten Commandments, held high in the air. He is exulting in the knowledge that the One coming out of the tomb fulfilled those laws to the letter. Jesus now transcends the commandments. He *is* the Word of God!

"The LORD would speak to Moses face to face, as one speaks to a friend."

EXODUS 33:11

On Moses' belt, I painted the Hebrew words for I AM (see Exodus 3:14; 6:2, 29). Because I haven't studied Hebrew, I needed help from someone who had. I called a local synagogue and asked if a rabbi could help me. When I received a return call, the rabbi asked if we could meet at a local "kosher" coffee shop. Feeling a bit like I was being drawn into a larger discussion, I reiterated that I only needed to have him write down the words in Hebrew and fax them to me. He insisted on meeting at the coffee shop. I gave in because I knew how important this would be to the painting.

The rabbi not only refused to write the words down for me, but informed me that I would not be able to write them either! The Jews believe that it is sacrilegious to write or even speak those words because they signify the very essence of God's character. When translated, I AM means something akin to God saying, *"I WAS, I AM, I ALWAYS WILL BE!"* The rabbi directed me instead to Exodus 20:2, where God gives the first of the Ten Commandments and God says, *"I am the LORD your God."* While these seem the same in English, the words in chapter 20 reveal a basic statement where God is matter-of-factly saying, "I am" your LORD. The "I am" statement there refers not to God's character but to His title. The Rabbi indicated the latter was acceptable to write and speak but not the former.

Obviously, this presented a problem for me. I was dealing with a very scholarly rabbi who brought up a rather good argument that was completely new to me. I can only attribute to the Holy Spirit what happened next. I said, "So, what you are telling me is that a person cannot speak those words, ever. Right?" Nodding, he said, "Yes!" I then asked him, "Well, then when God commanded Moses to say to Pharaoh & the Israelites that "I AM" had sent him, how did he do that if the words can't be spoken aloud or written?" After a pause, he said in a frustrated tone, "Uh, that was Moses!" I told him, "Sorry, I don't think it works like that!" Our conversation became even more heated. Up to that point, I had not yet told him what the mural was about, because I knew it would elicit a negative reaction from him. But when he began questioning me about it, I had no choice but to tell him that the subject was not Moses, but

Jesus. This, as you can imagine, did not go over well. When I told him that Jesus referred to Himself in John 8:58 using the exact same words found in Exodus chapters 3 and 6, he got the attention of all the people in the coffee shop when he raised his voice and said, "That's the problem with you Christians! You see the Old Testament through the New Testament and not the other way around!" I laughed to myself as I thought, "guilty as charged." Eventually, he came around and gave me what I needed, but I felt as though I had just gone 12 rounds with Mike Tyson!

In the mural, Moses is the first biblical figure on Christ's right-hand side, while Elijah is the first biblical figure on Christ's left-hand side. The placement of each was on purpose, since Scripture recounts that when Jesus was on the Mount of Transfiguration with Peter, James, and John, it was Moses and Elijah who met with Jesus there. I would love to know what they discussed. Whatever it was, Moses and Elijah were given a special treat to meet with Jesus, so in my mind that qualified them to be the closest in line to see Jesus as He reunites with His friends after conquering the grave!

Bill, a man from my church, was my model for Moses. Bill is a man of God who works with the homeless and destitute, caring for their material needs but always seeking to meet their spiritual needs. He not only looks like Moses, but he acts like Moses in his daily life. The costume for Bill was made simple by design. I don't think Moses would have approved of being cast as a man who would allow his apparel to distract from his words or lifestyle. Someday, I hope to ask him how close we came! Maybe he will even be wearing something very close to what I chose. How cool would that be? ■

"WHO AM I, THAT I SHOULD GO TO PHARAOH AND BRING THE ISRAELITES OUT OF EGYPT?"

EXODUS 3:11

ELIJAH

The Bible records that there are only two men who have never physically died. One is Enoch, whose departure sends a shiver up the spine of every believer who ever hopes to walk with God. Genesis 5:24 records it very simply: *And Enoch walked with God; and he was not, for God took him.* Oh, the days I have longed to switch places with Enoch. What can be compared to physically walking with God and then simply walking right into eternity with Him? In my opinion, nothing.

Elijah is the other man who never died, yet went to be with the Lord. His astounding departure is described in 2 Kings 2:11–12:

Then it came about as they were going along and talking, that behold, there appeared a chariot of fire and horses of fire which separated the two of them. And Elijah went up by a whirlwind to heaven. And Elisha saw it and cried out, "My father, my father, the chariots of Israel and its horsemen!" And he saw him no more.

Elijah went to be with God, never more to be seen until he was granted the honor of meeting with Jesus on the Mount of Transfiguration. After his spectacular exit from this world, only being in Jesus' presence was worth his return. When Jesus took Peter, James, and John up the mountain, He was transfigured into a glorious state right before them, and He shone like the sun. Even His garments shone white as light (see Matthew 17). The stunned apostles watched as two legendary figures, Moses and Elijah, appeared and met with Jesus. But make no mistake. This was not a meeting of three equals, though the apostles got confused for a moment. Peter blurted out, as only Peter could, *"Lord, it is good for us to be here; if you wish, I will put up three shelters—one for you, one for Moses and one for Elijah"* Matthew 17:4. Neither Moses nor Elijah responded to Peter, but Someone greater spoke to clear up Peter's confusion:

While he was still speaking, behold, a bright cloud overshadowed them; and behold, a voice out of the cloud, saying, "This is My Son, whom I love; with Him I am well pleased. Listen to Him!" Matthew 17:5. I can just hear the inflection in God's voice when He said the words *This*, *Son*, and *Him*.

I can almost see Moses and Elijah smile as they concurred with the voice of God. They knew that no one compares to Jesus! Jesus was not granted a favor by meeting with them; they were the recipients of the favor!

In the mural, I wanted Elijah to be as close to Jesus as he was on that mountain, so he is at the front of the line on Jesus' left side. Elijah, with hand raised, signals to Jesus, as though he is saying, "Here I am, Lord, I wouldn't have missed this for the world!"

When I studied Elijah, I saw a man who was rugged and determined. But throughout his amazing life and all the experiences he had while on the earth (even the tremendous miracles God did through him), he was just as human as the rest of us. After a scary run-in with Jezebel, King Ahab's evil wife, and fearing for his life, Elijah sat under a tree and wished to die (see 1 Kings 19). He basically said, "God, I'm done. Get me out of here. I can't stand this life any longer." Do you know what God did to help Elijah out of his funk and give him the strength to live? God placed him in a cave and spoke to him in a whisper!

Now Elijah stands before another cave and sees the greatest moment of all time. Once and for all, his Savior bursts out of a cave, confirming that He indeed is the Savior of the world.

How I found the model for Elijah is somewhat humorous. Needing some repair on my car, I took it to a local Midas Muffler dealer for a quote. While I was waiting, a mechanic walked out of the garage to the front office where I was sitting. It was Elijah! With one look, I knew I had found my model, so I wasted no time in seizing the moment. I stepped forward and asked if I could talk with him. Cautiously, he listened as I explained that he would make a wonderful model to photograph for my upcoming painting on the resurrection of Jesus Christ. I explained that I would like for him to pose as Elijah, if he would be willing. The first words out of his mouth were, "I'm Jewish!" But he asked his boss for time off for the day we were scheduled to photograph in Los Angeles. The manager agreed and Elijah was secured.

I thought the hard part was done, and I went on my way rejoicing at my good fortune. I didn't realize finding the costume would be a bigger challenge. My research convinced me that Elijah would have worn animal skins —something seen very unfavorably by many in our culture today — so finding suitable material was more than difficult. I eventually landed on a company that was able to get a full skin of an antelope that could have actually been from the very region Elijah came from! Although expensive, it was beautiful! And with that last piece, Elijah came to life before our very eyes. Most importantly, our Elijah model got introduced to the Savior of the world, Jesus! ■

THEN IT CAME ABOUT AS THEY WERE GOING ALONG AND TALKING, THAT BEHOLD, THERE APPEARED A CHARIOT OF FIRE AND HORSES OF FIRE WHICH SEPARATED THE TWO OF THEM. AND ELIJAH WENT UP BY A WHIRLWIND TO HEAVEN. AND ELISHA SAW IT AND CRIED OUT, "MY FATHER, MY FATHER, THE CHARIOTS OF ISRAEL AND ITS HORSEMEN!" AND HE SAW HIM NO MORE.

2 KINGS 2:11–12

NOAH

Besides Jesus, no character in the mural is better known than Noah. Even little children readily recognize Noah and his ark.

Noah, of course, lived before there was such a thing as rain, since God had covered the world in a blanket of dew from creation. (Some believe that the flood was actually a bursting of that canopy!) The Bible describes the state of affairs during Noah's day with a stark summary:

The LORD saw how great man's wickedness on the earth had become, and that every inclination of the thoughts of his heart was only evil all the time. Genesis 6:5.

Sadly, a quick look at the news today might cause us to draw the same conclusion about the day we are living in, don't you think?

Things were so bad in Noah's day that the LORD said: *"I will wipe mankind, whom I have created, from the face of the earth — men and animals, and creatures that move along the ground, and birds of the air — for I am grieved that I have made them."* Genesis 6:6–7.

For anyone who thinks it won't make a difference if one life is lived right within a culture of perversity, Genesis 6:8 clears up that mistaken notion:

But Noah found favor in the eyes of the LORD.

Most of you know the story well. God decided to make it rain torrentially on the earth for 40 days and 40 nights, thus destroying what He had made. But God gave the human race one more chance, telling Noah to make a huge boat and then put his family and two of every animal — male and female — into it and start all over again. This was no overnight event. It took Noah a lifetime (between 50-75 years) just to build the ark. During that time he was subjected to consistent mocking and ridicule for building a boat in preparation for the coming flood. Like Christians today who believe in things others cannot understand, Noah looked as if he were out of touch with reality. But just as surely as Noah knew there was a God, he knew that when God said something would happen, it would indeed happen. Not only did Noah have faith, he had an enormous amount of patience. He is the "poster boy" for everyone who needs a lesson in being patient while waiting for the fulfillment of the promises of God.

Living a life devoted to God has its ups and downs. Was there a time during all those years when Noah felt discouraged? Is it possible he began to doubt that it would ever rain, and that maybe he just heard wrong? Since the

Bible does not tell us, we cannot speculate that he did. However, we do know that if Noah did have doubts, they surely didn't keep him from working on the boat until it was completed.

Noah obeyed, and God made good on His promise. The day finally arrived. The LORD then said to Noah, *"Go into the ark, you and your whole family, because I have found you righteous in this generation."* Genesis 7:1. Animals were gathered in, scoffers were left outside laughing, and the rain began to pelt the earth. The rest, as they say, was history; and as always God was proven right.

This was the initial posing of Noah and Elijah side by side. I wanted to catch them awaiting the moment that Jesus appears from the tomb with the look of wonder and excitement that they surely had watching for the stone to roll away.

When I began the search for a Noah model, I couldn't help but think back to the movies I had seen throughout the years. I was most drawn to the movie *The Bible*, which featured Noah played by John Huston. I was influenced enough by that performance to recreate Noah from it. I made Noah a rugged man as well, wearing a simple, thick robe with few accessories.

When I started the photographing of Noah, played by a man from my church, I wanted to have him interact with Elijah, who was standing in front of him. I thought it might be interesting to show Noah and Elijah as if they had been discussing the moment before Jesus came out, and when that great moment appeared, Noah couldn't help but grab on to Elijah to get a better view and move him to one side. I thought it worked wonderfully, so when I sketched the mural out for approval and submitted it to the museum, I expected a favorable reaction. But the museum curators requested that the characters be separated in case we wanted to highlight them individually in print later on. Fittingly, Noah has both hands raised in the air, for he would have had the longest wait out of all the others to see God's promise fulfilled. If there were any discussion between Noah and Jesus after He came out of the tomb, I wonder if Noah received a special hug from Christ, since he was used by God to give man a second chance at life on earth? They surely both had that in common! ■

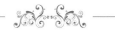

"The LORD saw how great man's wickedness on the earth had become, and that every inclination of the thoughts of his heart was only evil all the time."

GENESIS 6:5

THE LORD THEN SAID TO NOAH,
"GO INTO THE ARK, YOU AND YOUR WHOLE FAMILY, BECAUSE I HAVE FOUND YOU RIGHTEOUS IN THIS GENERATION."

GENESIS 7:1

ESTHER

As mentioned previously, the chance to include a woman in the mural was a breath of fresh air. Certainly God has used an abundance of women throughout history every bit as much as He used men; however, only one immediately came to mind as a genuine "Christ-type": Esther. She also had the greatest chance of instantly being recognized, since her queenly garb should help a viewer make the connection.

The story of Esther has been the subject of many movies over the years. I recently saw a movie called *One Night with the King*, which was created by the same company that provided the centurions' costumes I used in the mural! I studied that movie portrayal of Esther to get some ideas of age, general physical features, and what a queen might have worn.

Esther's story is truly a "rags to riches" story of one girl God used in a mighty way to save His people. An interesting note is that the name of God is never used throughout the entire book of Esther, yet His fingerprints are everywhere!

Esther lived during the time of Xerxes I, which was 486–465 BC. At that time Jerusalem was only a tiny outpost in the much greater empire that Xerxes ruled. Nevertheless, it played an extremely important role in the saving of God's people.

The residing queen, Vashti, made a decision to overrule her husband, King Xerxes. This action was contrary to the law of the land and an affront to the other leaders. Because it was done publicly, at a banquet, the king was put in a very awkward position. He had two options: he could do nothing and appear weak and not in control of his wife, or he could punish her severely as an example to everyone. On the insistence of the leaders, Xerxes took option number two. Vashti was summarily dismissed from ever coming in front of the king again. Xerxes decided to hold a beauty pageant to find Vashti's replacement.

It was then that a young Hebrew girl named Hadassah entered the story. For the sake of the pageant, Hadassah took the Persian name Esther, which means "star." And a star she was! After all the prospective candidates paraded before the king, none impressed him as much as the young Esther.

Esther was encouraged to join the pageant by her cousin Mordecai, who took her in as his own daughter when both of her parents died. Mordecai made it clear to Esther that she was not to admit her Hebrew background — the reason they chose a new name for her to take. Throughout the process, Mordecai would walk back and forth in front of the court of the harem to see how things were progressing for Esther (see Esther 2:11).

Xerxes chose Esther as his new queen. The Bible records: *Now the king was attracted to Esther more than to any of the other women, and she won his favor and approval more than any of the other virgins. So he set a royal crown on her head and made her queen instead of Vashti.* Esther 2:17

The king decided another banquet was in order, this time to celebrate his new queen, and announced it as Esther's banquet.

While Esther was vying for the title of queen, another story unfolded outside of the palace. As Mordecai sat at the king's gate, minding his own business, he overheard a plot to assassinate the king. He immediately told Esther, who informed the king. The perpetrators were caught and executed on the gallows. This event would become pivotal later in Mordecai's life.

Xerxes had an official named Haman, whom he promoted to high authority. Thus, when he rode through the town, all the people were expected to bow down in front of him to show honor. All did, except Mordecai, which put him squarely on Haman's enemies list. Now, Haman was such a narcissist that he could not, and would not, allow this affront to go unpunished. But he was afraid to arrest Mordecai because of the large Jewish population. So he planned to destroy Mordecai along with all the Jews. Talk about an overreaction!

The next events in the story prove that no one can stand against God. Haman decided to make a veiled demand of the king, to issue what first appeared as a harmless decree on the king's behalf. He asked for a decree that would require that any people (the Jews) who followed any law other than the laws of Persia be annihilated. This sounded good to the king, so he signed the decree and gave his royal signet ring to Haman as a sign of ultimate authority. Haman made sure that every province received the decree in writing, and it was posted everywhere. Upon hearing this, Mordecai and all the Jews in every Persian town began to mourn.

Esther got wind of Mordecai's sorrow and sought to get to the bottom of it. Through an intermediary, she learned what Mordecai knew and was informed that he was asking her to go to the king to stop the evil Haman. Esther refused telling Mordecai that, according to the law, she didn't have the ability to just show up before the king anytime she wanted to. But Mordecai's famous response followed:

"Do not think that because you are in the king's house you alone of all the Jews will escape. For if you remain silent at this time, relief and deliverance for the Jews will arise from another place, but you and your father's family will perish. And who knows but that you have come to royal position for such a time as this?" Esther 4:13–14

Mordecai's words fell heavily on Esther's heart and conscience. She would go before the king, invited or not. This is where the greatest statement Esther ever uttered shows her to be a Christ-type:

"Go, gather together all the Jews who are in Susa, and fast for me. Do not eat or drink for three days, night or day. I and my maids will fast as you do. When this is done, I will go to the king, even though it is against the law. ***And if I perish, I perish****"* Esther 4:16 (emphasis mine).

Today, as Christians, many would have caved in to the pressure Esther found herself under and would have found a million excuses to get out from the potentially deadly responsibility. Esther didn't have the advantage of the New Testament, where Jesus shows us how to say, as He did in the Garden of Gethsemane, *"My Father, if it is possible, may this cup be taken from me. Yet not as I will, but as you will"* Matthew 26:39. However, Esther's version was pretty close! Though young, she showed the faith, wisdom, and maturity of someone much more advanced. Esther was willing to die to save her people.

We all know the events that followed; Esther was spared, the Jewish people saved, evil Haman punished, and Mordecai honored in spectacular fashion. Once again, perfect cascade of events only God could have orchestrated.

And now, kneeling before the tomb, Esther watches as her Hero, the One who did in fact die to save the people, comes back to life.

Our church also provided the model for Esther, in the form of a beautiful girl named Jessica. During the modeling shoot, she became faint and alerted me that she had a condition that caused her to faint without warning. For a brief moment, I panicked, thinking I may have made a mistake in choosing her. But she persevered, got up off the couch, and finished the photo shoot — with the determination of Esther. ■

NOW THE KING WAS ATTRACTED TO ESTHER MORE THAN TO ANY OF THE OTHER WOMEN, AND SHE WON HIS FAVOR AND APPROVAL MORE THAN ANY OF THE OTHER VIRGINS. SO HE SET A ROYAL CROWN ON HER HEAD AND MADE HER QUEEN INSTEAD OF VASHTI.

ESTHER 2:17

JOHN THE BAPTIST

Of all the human characters in the mural, I think that I identify with John the most. John was the cousin of Jesus and served as the "forerunner" of Christ. He played a huge part in the New Testament and yet never took any glory or credit for himself.

John's parents were Zechariah and Elizabeth. Zechariah was a priest in the temple, and Elizabeth was from the line of Aaron. The Bible describes them as both *"upright in the sight of God, observing all the Lord's commandments and regulations blamelessly"* Luke 1:6. Both Zechariah and Elizabeth were advanced in years, and Elizabeth was barren. But God had a plan for them and for their soon to arrive son John.

Zechariah was chosen by lot to offer incense at the altar of incense, a priestly duty which was granted but once in the life of a priest. As he stood at the altar, something momentous happened — the angel Gabriel appeared to him with great news:

"Do not be afraid, Zechariah; your prayer has been heard. Your wife Elizabeth will bear you a son, and you are to give him the name John. He will be a joy and delight to you, and many will rejoice because of his birth, for he will be great in the sight of the Lord. He is never to take wine or other fermented drink, and he will be filled with the Holy Spirit even from birth. Many of the people of Israel will he bring back to the Lord their God. And he will go on before the Lord, in the spirit and power of Elijah, to turn the hearts of the fathers to their children and the disobedient to the wisdom of the righteous — to make ready a people prepared for the Lord". Luke 1:13–17.

It's clear that Zechariah was overwhelmed. As most people are prone to do when overwhelmed, he didn't say the right thing at the right time. He asked Gabriel, *"How can I be sure of this? I am an old man and my wife is well along in years".* Luke 1:18

Zechariah's question would seem harmless to most people, but God saw what was in his heart. Gabriel discerned that Zechariah doubted, so he pronounced the verdict:

"I am Gabriel. I stand in the presence of God, and I have been sent to speak to you and to tell you this good news. And now you will be silent and not able to speak until the day this happens, because you did not believe my words, which will come true at their proper time". Luke 1:19–20

Sure enough, it happened exactly as Gabriel said, and Zechariah had to exit the temple without the ability to communicate. This made the people realize that he had seen a vision while performing his duties.

Just as Gabriel said, Elizabeth became pregnant. Here the Bible says something it doesn't explain: it records that Elizabeth kept herself in seclusion for five months. Was she ill? Did she simply not want to jeopardize her pregnancy by too much activity? I guess we will have to wait to ask her when we get to heaven!

The miracles for Elizabeth continued as a surprise visit from Mary confirmed what the angel Gabriel told her about the Holy Spirit filling her baby even in the womb. Elizabeth recounted the moment Mary spoke to her: *"As soon as the sound of your greeting reached my ears, the baby in my womb leaped for joy"* Luke 1:44. Even then, John responded to the Savior. From the womb, his life would be devoted to hearing the Savior's voice.

John's start was miraculous in every sense of the word, but his life would not be an easy one. Right away, John found himself training in the lonely desert wilderness. When he entered the towns, he preached *"a baptism of repentance for the forgiveness of sins."* Luke 3:3. That was hardly what the people wanted to hear (and not what they want to hear even today)! John's language was less than cordial most of the time, and it normally elicited anger and argument from the ranking people of his day.

While controversial, John was also humbly prophetic. When the crowds wanted to know if he was the promised Christ, John answered emphatically:

"I baptize you with water. But one more powerful than I will come, the thongs of whose sandals I am not worthy to untie. He will baptize you with the Holy Spirit and with fire". Luke 3:16

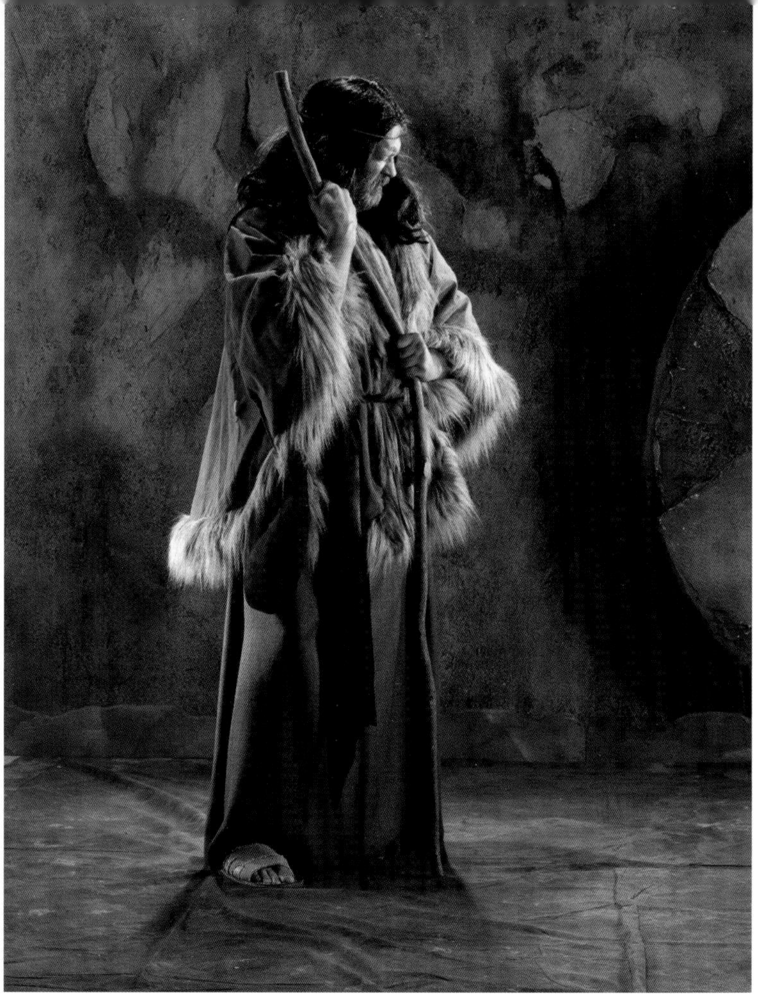

Filling the shoes of John the Baptist was no small task. My fellow artist and brother in Christ, Chris Hopkins, traveled a long way to model for the mural. This was another alternate posing we explored.

"Look, the Lamb of God,
who takes away the sin of the world!"
JOHN 1:29

On one particular day, John looked up to see someone who once again made his heart leap as it did when he was in his mother's womb. Jesus came to John to be baptized, and as John realized the enormity of the moment, he tried to put things into context by saying:

*"**I** need to be baptized by **you**, and do you come to **me**?" But Jesus answered him, saying, "Let it be so now; it is proper for us to do this to fulfill all righteousness"* Matthew 3:14–15, (emphasis mine).

When John baptized Him ... heaven was opened and the Holy Spirit descended on him in bodily form like a dove. And a voice came from heaven: *"You are my Son, whom I love; with you I am well pleased"*. Luke 3:21–22

Through this baptism experience, John had the privilege of marking the beginning of Jesus' earthly ministry. His job of paving the way as a forerunner was done. He had announced Jesus' coming to the world with these words: *"Look, the Lamb of God, who takes away the sin of the world!"* John 1:29.

Shortly after Jesus' baptism, the Bible records that John was imprisoned for his declarations of the sins of Herod. His arrest is not as startling as what happened to him in prison. He became discouraged and confused. His vision had been crystal clear as to who Jesus was. After all, he had baptized Him and announced His coming! But while in prison, his vision became clouded. Ever been there? I have. That's why I so identify with John. But John didn't wallow in his doubt and despair. He went right back to the source. He sent some of his disciples to ask Jesus one simple question: *"Are You the one who was to come, or should we expect someone else?"* Luke 7:19. Those are the questions that despairing circumstances will always cause us to ask. *"God, are You who I thought You were, or was that just my hope that You were all those things?"*

"I tell you, among those born of women there is no one greater than John; yet the one who is least in the kingdom of God is greater than he."

LUKE 7:28

Jesus did not slap His forehead and get upset with John's question. He didn't say to John, "You've got to be kidding me. After all this time, and all you saw, you doubt? Give me a break!" Despairing circumstances will sometimes cause us to ask God, "Are You who *I thought You were?"* Just like today, when you and I get confused because of life's hurting circumstances and God seems nowhere to be found, Jesus points us back to the proof that cannot be denied. Jesus' response to John's question is all the proof we need:

"Go back and report to John what you have seen and heard: The blind receive sight, the lame walk, those who have leprosy are cured, the deaf hear, the dead are raised, and the good news is preached to the poor. Blessed is the man who does not fall away on account of me." Luke 7:22

Jesus did not rush to see John in prison for a special visit. Instead, He simply pointed to the undeniable truth. Some scholars have defended John by pointing out that while he knew all the miracles that Jesus was foretold to perform, he never had a chance to see them with his own eyes because he was thrown into prison. But whatever the reason for John's confusion, he got the answer he needed, and it carried him through all the way to the moment Herod killed him.

Jesus still cares enough today to provide us with what we need in order to straighten out our confusion. Like us, John had to believe in what Jesus said and let His words be all the proof he needed.

John now stands outside Jesus' tomb with absolute proof of what Jesus said and did. Now the ultimate act is before John's eyes. I tried to paint John a bit sorrowful, because of the moments when he doubted. That helps us identify with him. I know that when I doubt, and Jesus winds up coming through wonderfully on my behalf, the aftermath of it is sorrow. I am disappointed in myself for allowing circumstances to blur His face from me.

Before we reach a hard conclusion on John, let's hear from Jesus first. This is what Jesus said about John to the crowds:

"I tell you, among those born of women there is no one greater than John; yet the one who is least in the kingdom of God is greater than he." Luke 7:28

The model for John is my good friend and great fellow artist, Chris Hopkins. Chris, a brother in Christ, traveled a long way to help me and really fell into the role of John quite naturally. Again, I didn't have to provide much art direction, thankfully!

However, when I needed to outfit John, I found that it was more difficult than I thought. The Scripture describes John's clothing as *"made of camel's hair, and he had a leather belt around his waist"* (Matthew 3:4). The belt was no problem, but when I tried to get a skin of camel's hair, the closest I could come to it was some fabric that emulated it. Thankfully, it came off better than I could have hoped! ■

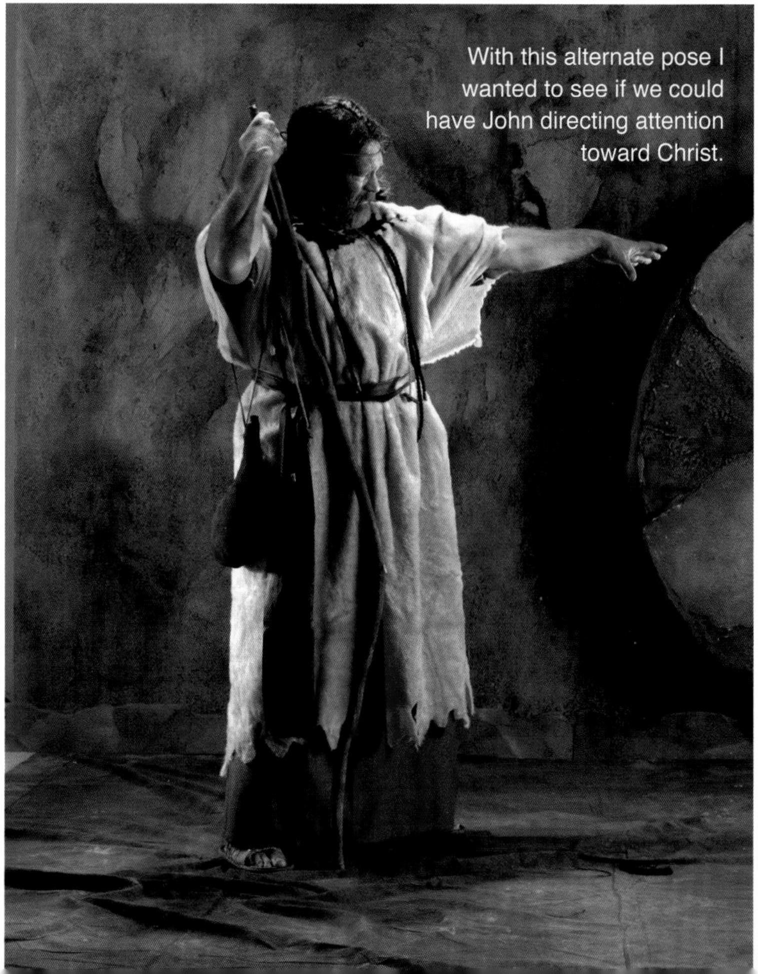

With this alternate pose I wanted to see if we could have John directing attention toward Christ.

I TELL YOU, AMONG THOSE BORN OF WOMEN THERE IS NO ONE GREATER THAN JOHN; YET THE ONE WHO IS LEAST IN THE KINGDOM OF GOD IS GREATER THAN HE.

LUKE 7:28

DANIEL

The final figure in the cloud of witnesses is Daniel, the one who is famous for surviving the lion's den. Daniel is a magnificent example of what God can do through a man who is yielded to Him.

Early in his life, Daniel came to an important conclusion about how he would live. When the Babylonians "drafted" young Israelite youths to be trained and eventually serve in their government, Daniel was chosen to go. However, he didn't let the honor go to his head or change his beliefs. He honored God in every part of his life, including in his choices of what to eat.

But Daniel resolved not to defile himself with the royal food and wine, and he asked the chief official for permission not to defile himself this way. Daniel 1:8

When Daniel held strong to his beliefs, God gave him favor even with those responsible for his training. The evaluation of Daniel after all was said and done was that Daniel came out head and shoulders above all the other candidates. Daniel eventually became a high-ranking official in the government of his time. He was first a commissioner. Then, after he interpreted the handwriting that God put on the wall during one of King Belshazzar's self-indulgent parties, Daniel was elevated to the rank of third in the kingdom — although that would be a short-lived position, since the next day the king died and Darius took the throne.

Did this mean Daniel had it easy? Was it straight to the top of the food chain? Not hardly. Daniel (just like David, Esther, John, and so many others) found out that his promotions were opportunities for God to use him, but his detractors would be many. Even with his high standing in the kingdom, Daniel, along with his three friends, was tested to the ultimate degree.

Daniel was tested over and over by the king when it came to interpreting dreams and visions that troubled him. Each time, God gave Daniel all the answers, and Daniel gave God all the credit. Even still, the king would return to pagan rituals, and Daniel would be placed on the "hot seat" more than once.

The most famous of these trials is well known to many as "Daniel in the lions' den." Because Daniel got promoted, there were a lot of angry men who tried to find a way to trap Daniel in an error. So they cooked up a scheme that started with an observation of Daniel. They saw that he prayed to God. Going behind his back, they approached the king with what looked like an innocent proclamation for the king to decree. Put simply, they wanted the king to sign a petition stating that anyone who prayed to someone other than him would be thrown into the lions' den.

The king didn't see the long-term consequences and signed the decree, only to realize that he had trapped himself into a scheme that even he couldn't rescind. Daniel's enemies waited to see what Daniel would do now that he was prohibited from praying to God.

Daniel did exactly as they had hoped. As soon as Daniel found out about the signed decree, the Bible tells us he:

...went home to his upstairs room where the windows opened toward Jerusalem ... got down on his knees and prayed, giving thanks to his God, just as he had done before. Daniel 6:10

As you can imagine, his enemies went straight to the king and demanded that he stand behind his decree. The king knew he had been had, but it was too late to undo what was done. Even though distressed, he had to command Daniel to be thrown into the lions' den. The king was so upset that he couldn't sleep and spent the night fasting for Daniel. Early the next morning...

... the King got up and hurried to the lions' den. When he came near the den, he called to Daniel in an anguished voice, "Daniel, servant of the living God, has your God, whom you serve continually, been able to rescue you from the lions?" Daniel 6:19–20

I don't know if Daniel's response was instantaneous, but it must have felt like an eternity to the king before he heard Daniel's voice saying:

"My God sent his angel, and he shut the mouths of the lions. They have not hurt me, because I was found innocent in his sight. Nor have I ever done any wrong before you, O king." Daniel 6:22

"My God sent his angel, and he shut the mouths of the lions. They have not hurt me, because I was found innocent in his sight. Nor have I ever done any wrong before you, O king."

DANIEL 6:22

I have often wondered if Daniel was frightened throughout that night. It would not have been unreasonable, given the circumstances. Some people without faith might argue that the lions just weren't hungry that night. But we know from Scripture that those lions were starving.

"At the king's command, the men who had falsely accused Daniel were brought in and thrown into the lions' den, along with their wives and children. And before they reached the floor of the den, the lions overpowered them and crushed all their bones." Daniel 6:24

Daniel continued to walk with God and was given much insight into spiritual matters. He was given a behind-the-curtain view of what spiritual warfare looks like by the angel Gabriel. For the rest of Daniel's life, God revealed to him details about the end times. Scholars have said that every chapter of Daniel is either quoted in or alluded to in the book of Revelation, and only two chapters in Revelation are without some background in Daniel!

To read the last few chapters of Daniel is like reading today's headlines in the newspaper. Some events have already happened, and events to come are not pretty at all — except for the resurrection of the dead, described in Daniel 12:1–3.

"At that time Michael, the great prince who protects your people, will arise. There will be a time of distress such as has not happened from the beginning of nations until then. But at that time your people—everyone whose name is found written in the book—will be delivered. Multitudes who sleep in the dust of the earth will awake: some to everlasting life, others to shame and everlasting contempt. Those who are wise will shine like the brightness of the heavens, and those who lead many to righteousness, like the stars for ever and ever."

In the mural, I have shown Daniel kneeling at the tomb with his head down in prayer, just as he was in life. Like the other two royal people, David and Esther, Daniel knows to whom all the credit belongs. Because Daniel was given such insight into the resurrection of the dead, I can only imagine the thoughts going through his mind at seeing the One rising from the dead, the One who makes it all possible!

Our church provided the model for Daniel. It wasn't until I read the entire book of Daniel that I realized that God had helped me typecast Daniel perfectly! ■

BUT DANIEL RESOLVED NOT TO DEFILE HIMSELF WITH THE ROYAL FOOD AND WINE, AND HE ASKED THE CHIEF OFFICIAL FOR PERMISSION NOT TO DEFILE HIMSELF THIS WAY.

DANIEL 1:8

THE GUARDS

As could have been predicted, the leaders who crucified Jesus didn't stop there. They were determined to rid the world of Jesus and His followers. They remembered what Jesus had said when He talked about His death and resurrection. So they took all the proper precautions after Jesus was crucified to make sure no one messed with their plans.

The next day, the one after Preparation Day, the chief priests and the Pharisees went to Pilate. "Sir," they said, "we remember that while he was still alive that deceiver said, 'After three days I will rise again.' So give the order for the tomb to be made secure until the third day. Otherwise, his disciples may come and steal the body and tell the people that he has been raised from the dead. This last deception will be worse than the first."

"Take a guard," Pilate answered. "Go, make the tomb as secure as you know how." So they went and made the tomb secure by putting a seal on the stone and posting the guard.
Matthew 27:62–66

Do you sense the fear in a bunch of people who have the feeling that Jesus might just be who He said He was? After all, nobody puts a fence around a cemetery to keep the people in! The story continued to unfold.

Do you sense the fear in a bunch of people who have the feeling that Jesus might just be who He said He was?

After the Sabbath, at dawn on the first day of the week, Mary Magdalene and the other Mary went to look at the tomb. There was a violent earthquake, for an angel of the Lord came down from heaven and, going to the tomb, rolled back the stone and sat on it. His appearance was like lightning, and his clothes were white as snow. The guards were so afraid of him that they shook and became like dead men.
Matthew 28:1–4

The leaders' worst nightmare came true, and it was more spectacular than they could guard against. All their best efforts could not stop even one of God's angels. They could have had the entire Roman army and it would have made no difference. Somehow, I suspect they knew that their efforts would result in a lost cause from the very start!

I painted the guards lying prostrate in a dead faint on the ground. As you might have noticed, the guards, the angels, and Christ are painted in full opaque color, as they are all in the human dimension — unlike the "cloud of witnesses" who are ghosted in places, showing they are in the supernatural realm.

Look at the ground between the two guards and you will notice that I painted it splitting from the earthquake mentioned in the above Scripture passage.

I used two of our music ministers from church, Ricardo and Nick, to pose as the guards. (Lucky for them, they had the easiest poses of all the models!) ■

AFTER THE SABBATH, AT DAWN ON THE FIRST DAY OF THE WEEK, MARY MAGDALENE AND THE OTHER MARY WENT TO LOOK AT THE TOMB. THERE WAS A VIOLENT EARTHQUAKE, FOR AN ANGEL OF THE LORD CAME DOWN FROM HEAVEN AND, GOING TO THE TOMB, ROLLED BACK THE STONE AND SAT ON IT. HIS APPEARANCE WAS LIKE LIGHTNING, AND HIS CLOTHES WERE WHITE AS SNOW. THE GUARDS WERE SO AFRAID OF HIM THAT THEY SHOOK AND BECAME LIKE DEAD MEN.

MATTHEW 29:1–4

THE ANGELS

For many years, I have used angels in my paintings and have pictured them in a variety of ways. One day, I came across a writing that has forever transformed my thinking about angels.

First, I learned that there is no such thing as a female angel (sorry, all you manufacturers and gift distributors out there) and while the general public may like to see the chubby little angel-like Cupid with the small wings hovering above two starstruck lovers, that depiction of angels is not biblically accurate either. Many have even called those little angels "cherubs" or "cherubim." A more accurate description of cherubim comes from Genesis 3:34. God placed cherubim at the entrance to the Garden of Eden after the expulsion of Adam and Eve. The cherubim were the final defense against reentry to the Garden of Eden! I seriously doubt that a little baby angel with tiny wings would have dissuaded them!

Cherubim served God in different ways. The psalmist described one way:

[God] parted the heavens and came down; dark clouds were under his feet. He mounted the cherubim and flew; he soared on the wings of the wind. Psalms 18:9–10

Doesn't exactly sound like a wimpy or feminine angel, does it?

Second, I learned that every time an angel approaches a person in the Bible, the result is fear or dread in the one who is approached. In fact, most of the encounters with angels in the Bible are followed with some variation of the words "Do not fear!" No flying baby could generate such a response!

Over the years I have also learned that although some people are against the idea of showing angels with wings, the Bible describes angels as having them. For example, Ezekiel clearly identified the cherubim he saw as having four wings (see Ezekiel 1). Also, when the Ark of the Covenant was made, winged cherubim adorned the top of it (see Exodus 37:9).

One truth about angels that is very clear in the Bible is that they are created beings. God never intended for them to be worshipped, nor are we ever commanded to pray to them. It is God who dispatches them at His disposal to do His will. Colossians 2:18 tells us:

Do not let anyone who delights in false humility and the worship of angels disqualify you for the prize. Such a person goes into great detail about what he has seen, and his unspiritual mind puffs him up with idle notions.

Angels are commissioned by God to do His will as well as to protect us. They are *"ministering spirits sent to serve those who will inherit salvation."* Hebrews 1:14. However, angels find their greatest satisfaction and delight in worshipping God. Nearly the entire book of Revelation is filled with verses that describe the awe and delight that the angels have when this is their function. This is beautifully expressed in the words of Revelation 4:8:

Day and night they never stop saying: "Holy, holy, holy is the Lord God Almighty, who was, and is, and is to come."

When it came to showing angels at the Resurrection, I did not consider it my aim to be "documentary" in how I pictured them. My primary concern was, and continues to be, to show that angels attend Christ, just as they did when He suffered in the wilderness while being tempted by the devil (see Matthew 4:11).

[God] parted the heavens and came down; dark clouds were under his feet. He mounted the cherubim and flew; he soared on the wings of the wind.

PSALMS 18:9-10

My imagination ran wild with ideas of how to best present these angels who would have been dispatched to honor the moment of Jesus' resurrection from the dead. I tried to show them in splendor: brilliant and with militaristic clothing. You may even see the epaulettes on their shoulders, with the gold braiding cascading down their arms. Heaven's best were dispatched, for sure. I'm thinking that there must have been a legion of angels who asked for the privilege of being there, but only two were chosen. I may have unconsciously thought of the two being Gabriel and Michael. Use your imagination to see that the others are somewhere in the foreground, by the thousands, each just trying to get a peek at the risen Savior!

In my sketches for the angels, I think I tried too hard to make them look important. I first tried showing them standing, holding swords that touched up above Christ's head. The idea came from what knights used to do in medieval times when a king would walk under their swords. After I put them in the sketch, the result was that it looked as though they were about to bring the swords down on Jesus' head, so that idea quickly got nixed!

My next attempt was to show them standing and holding torches of fire as Christ emerged. I must have been subliminally picturing the Holy Spirit being symbolized through the fire. The torches became so important that they actually took away attention from Christ, which would have been the last thing I wanted to do. So that went away as well.

My final attempt was to show the angels kneeling, with swords and with bowed heads. (I'm told that it is considered improper for a subordinate to look directly into the eyes of royalty.) I felt that was a good way to show the ultimate respect that the angels would have had for Christ, since they knew Him throughout the ages as the King of kings who had descended to earth as a baby, not just to be born, but to die and be placed in a borrowed tomb. Coming out of that tomb, they once again honor Him as the King of kings, and there is no other posture to take but on bended knee. You may detect a slight smile on their faces, which I put there on purpose. I would think that if they could show it, they were swelling with pride and admiration for their King!

Look closely at the swords of the angels. On the top of each of the swords is The Star Of David. Down on the actual metal shafts of the swords are two Greek symbols. The angel on the left of the painting has the symbol of Alpha, and the angel on the right has the symbol of Omega. These are the beginning and ending letters of the Greek alphabet. They are, more importantly, ancient references to Christ being the beginning and the end of all things!

The models were two young men I have used as angels on previous occasions. Since we had a history together, they needed the least amount of direction in posing. They fell into their poses as naturally as they had in the past photo shoots we had done together. It actually was refreshing to not have to "think" for them, but allow them to bring something to the scene themselves that worked as well as it did! ■

THE RESURRECTED JESUS

You may wonder why I left the chapter on Christ for the very last. My only answer is an old one: "I saved the best for last!" Up to now, everyone and everything else has been "window dressing," so to speak. Not that they aren't important, but compared to Jesus they really were optional! Even as I write this, a million thoughts flood my mind, and I cannot write fast enough to get it all down. There is so much to say. So I will take a deep breath, and here goes…

Quite frankly, the resurrection of Jesus Christ is the single most important act in the history of mankind.

The nativity was of utmost importance to the world and certainly worth the celebration we call Christmas.

The miracles Jesus performed have never been equaled and certainly validated Him as the prophesied Son of God. These were not only needed, but they were also spectacular beyond our wildest imagination. Only Jesus ever could do the things He did.

Isaiah predicted the crucifixion of Christ 700 years before it happened. The prophetic words in Isaiah 53:3–5 let us in on God's plan to save people:

He was despised and rejected by men,
a man of sorrows, and familiar with suffering.
Like one from whom men hide their faces
He was despised, and we esteemed Him not.
Surely he took up our infirmities
and carried our sorrows,
yet we considered Him stricken by God,
smitten by Him, and afflicted.
But He was pierced for our transgressions,
He was crushed for our iniquities;
the punishment that brought us peace was upon Him,
and by His wounds we are healed.

What a description! Jesus bore that for you and me. Many who saw *The Passion of the Christ* were appalled at the torture administered to Jesus. But what Jesus actually endured was much, much worse. Even the makers of the movie admitted that it was much worse in reality, but they felt that what they did show was all that the viewers would be able to take! The reality is that Jesus' body *"was so disfigured beyond that of any man and his form marred beyond human likeness"* Isaiah 52:14.

Even so, the crucifixion would not have completed God's plan. Jesus did die for us, but in His death alone there is no guarantee of life beyond the grave. The apostle Paul tells us that *"if Christ has not been raised, our preaching is useless and so is your faith"* 1 Corinthians 15:14. Did you get that? Everything Jesus did up to that point had to culminate in something more. That something more is the Resurrection!

On Easter Sunday, we ought to be dancing in the streets with excitement! Our joy should be at its apex when we think of the Resurrection! Do you realize that while other religions may have good philosophies, and other belief systems encourage noble acts of service, only Christianity has a Savior! Jesus tells this to us in John 14:6. *"I am the way and the truth and the life. No one comes to the Father except through me."* That has to be the most narrow-minded statement I have ever heard in my life. But truth is narrow-minded, isn't it?

Unfortunately, many people have relegated the resurrection of Jesus to what we call the Easter season. Some even go so far as to tell the "Easter story." Let me remind you that it is no story at all but a true event! Over 500 people saw Jesus after He rose from the dead. In any court of law, then or now, the testimony of two witnesses who agree is taken for truth. If two can be considered true testimony, then what do 500 account for?

In our lives, the Resurrection must be a daily remembrance of what Jesus did for us. No one else could have been the perfect, spotless Lamb of God who took away our sins. No one else could have sealed it all with a final drubbing of death! He soundly defeated Satan, who thought he had devised the perfect plan to kill and get rid of Jesus once and for all. I imagine that while the arrest of Jesus and the crucifixion were taking place, the devil and his miserable cohorts must have been gleefully celebrating that they would win the war by killing Jesus on the cross. Little did they know that the only thing they did was help fulfill God's plan to save the world! I wish I could have seen the looks on their twisted faces when they heard the footsteps of Jesus stepping from the grave above and coming down to confront the devil to take the keys of death and hell from Satan (see Revelation 1:18). I don't envision Jesus politely asking for the keys. I see Him taking hold of them and ripping them from Satan's death grip, saying, "These are mine!"

Then I imagine Satan crawling away, back to whatever hole he crawled out from, to weep for eternity. He not only lost, but lost spectacularly! Now the best Satan can hope for is that you and I will not remember this fateful day, so he can try to fool us into thinking that he is still able to put us into hell with him forever. Not a chance! Not after the Resurrection! When we accept Christ as Savior we're guaranteed eternity in Heaven!

Do you realize the magnitude of what Jesus did by rising from the dead? Do you know Him as your Lord and Savior? Do you bow your knee in prayer and devote your life to

Him so that you can live for Him now and have forever with Him later? If yes, then you are on the winning side! Rejoice!

Through Christ's resurrection, we are given life. Jesus said, *"I am the resurrection and the life"* John 11:25. It may surprise some people to know that Jesus actually spoke those words before His crucifixion and subsequent resurrection!

Jesus had a dear friend named Lazarus that appears in Scripture. Lazarus' sisters, Mary and Martha, were also devoted followers of Jesus. They lived in a town called Bethany. On one particular day when Jesus was away, Lazarus became sick.

After Mary and Martha sent someone to tell Jesus of His friend's sickness, Jesus responded by saying, *"This sickness will not end in death. No, it is for God's glory so that God's Son may be glorified through it"* John 11:4. But later Jesus told His disciples who were with Him, *"Lazarus is dead, and for your sake I am glad I was not there, so that you may believe. But let us go to him"* John 11:14–15.

The disciples didn't understand. Jesus said plainly that Lazarus wasn't going to die, and then later said that Lazarus had died. Was Jesus confused? Did He just change His mind? Like all of us who ever think Jesus played a trick on us or forgot what He promised us, the confused disciples were about to find that Jesus was way ahead of them —again!

When Jesus arrived in Bethany, Lazarus had already been rotting in a grave for four days. Needless to say, the two sisters were baffled as to why Jesus hadn't arrived sooner. Mary stayed home (probably angry at Jesus for not showing up sooner), but Martha immediately went to Jesus and said, *"Lord, if you had been here, my brother would not have died."* John 11:21.

Jesus then said to Martha, *"Your brother will rise again"* John 11:23. Martha assumed Jesus was referring to the last days, but what she really wanted was for her brother to be alive that very moment! This was the context in which Jesus spoke those powerful words and claimed:

"I am the resurrection and the life. He who believes in me will live, even though he dies; and whoever lives and believes in me will never die. Do you believe this?" John 11:25–26

> *"I believe that you are the Christ, the Son of God, who was to come into the world."*
>
> JOHN 11:27

Martha was faced with the choice to believe or not to believe. She believed and spoke these words: *"I believe that you are the Christ, the Son of God, who was to come into the world"* John 11:27.

Mary finally realized that it was time to go to Jesus, so she made her way to Him, saying *"Lord, if you had been here, my brother would not have died."* John 11:32. Déjà vu, all over again! But did Jesus get angry? No. He instead asked to be led to where Lazarus was buried.

Martha, always the practical one, reminded Jesus that Lazarus had been dead for four days and that his body wouldn't smell so good! But just as I mentioned earlier, in the stories of Elijah and David, God seems to do His best work in caves! John 11:41–44 describes what happened next better than I could.

Jesus looked up and said, "Father, I thank you that you have heard me. I knew that you always hear me, but I said this for the benefit of the people standing here, that they may believe that you sent me."

When he had said this, Jesus called in a loud voice, "Lazarus, come out!" The dead man came out, his hands and feet wrapped with strips of linen, and a cloth around his face.

Jesus said to them, "Take off the grave clothes and let him go."

Wow! Now do you get it? Jesus had resurrection power flowing through Him even before He came out of His own tomb! Hebrews 13:8 says that *"Jesus Christ is the same yesterday and today and forever."* If that is true, that He is the same today as He was then, and He lives within me, then why do I sometimes seem so powerless? I hate to answer my own question, but here's the conclusion I have come to: I am Mary, and I am Martha, and I am the Jews who criticized Jesus. I am better at whining than I am at believing, so I get exactly what I deserve — nothing. No power to do anything. I sometimes forget one of the most important passages in the Bible:

But when he asks, he must believe and not doubt, because he who doubts is like a wave of the sea, blown and tossed by the wind. That man should not think he will receive anything from the Lord; he is a double-minded man, unstable in all he does.

James 1:6–8

Thankfully, I'm not always so unbelieving! When I was painting the mural, there were times I got so choked up at what the Lord had done for me that I would begin to weep. The realization would set in that I can live with that same resurrection power Jesus lived with, and I don't have to be a victim of this world that Jesus conquered. I remember one time when I was crying (while suspended 15 feet in the air on a scissor lift) and I said, "God if I don't stop crying, I'm not going to be able to finish this!" As quickly as I said it, I heard that still, small voice of God say to me, "Don't worry, you are not doing it anyway!" Ha!

"Jesus Christ is the same yesterday and today and forever."

HEBREWS 13:8

There were times during the process of this monumental task that I truly experienced resurrection power, because there is no way I could have done this work by myself. I know me — and I'm not that good!

The very first brushstrokes I put on the mural were on the face of Christ. His face is the centerpiece of the painting, so I knew that if it didn't come out right, then I probably should just stop right there and bag the whole thing!

As I painted Christ's face, my desire was to make sure that I did more than just a good portrait of Jesus. I wanted His eyes to be looking up, to the Father, at that moment of emerging, as if to say, *"Father, I did it! I did what You asked of Me. It's over! I saved Your children! I am coming Home!"*

After I painted Jesus' face, I remember being euphoric

that it actually came out as I had hoped! That was the moment I knew God was in this depiction and that He would hold my hand and move the brush along throughout the entire process!

As I painted the immediate background behind Christ's head, I wanted to get some of the texture of the stone to be prominent. As I started to scrub the area with brushstrokes, I realized that the strokes were beginning to take on the look of thorns! The crown of thorns Jesus wore for us! When things like that happen to me, I remember who is really painting the mural, for that element was not in my plans but turned out to be a crucial part of the mural!

Looking further down on Christ's body, you can see that I gave Him the gown of a King, fittingly so. My goal was not to say that I know what Christ's garment looked like when He exited the tomb. It was my desire, however, to remind the viewer that no matter what He wore, He exited as a King!

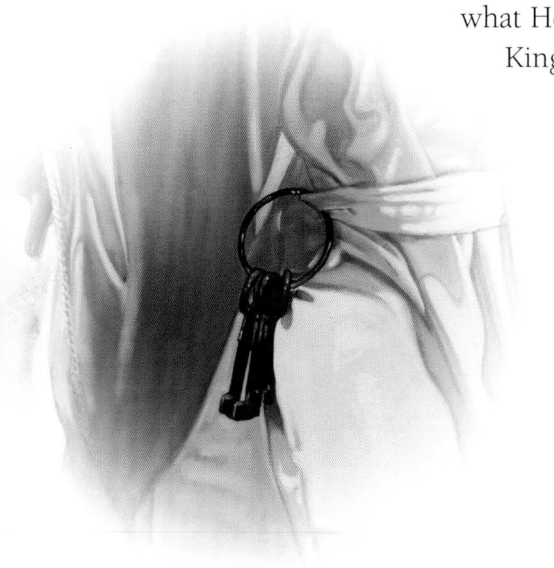

You will notice on His belt are a set of keys. These are the keys referred to earlier that are mentioned in Revelation 1:18.

Look at Christ's hands. In this moment, Jesus might have touched the outside of the tomb as he stepped forth, and in doing so, I imagined the power that must have emanated from Him. I used the equivalent of modern-day laser beams to give the viewer the sense of the visible power of God. (For those of you who may point out that the Bible doesn't mention laser beams, let me remind you that God knew about laser beams long before the world was created!) Notice also that there are no nail marks on Christ's hands. In studying, I found that the nail marks would have been in His wrists, as that would have been the only part capable of withstanding the weight of his body as He hung on the Cross. Since the sleeves of the garment are over His wrists, the nail marks are not visible.

Look just to the right of Christ, and you will see a window in the tomb. Many have asked the significance of that window. All I know is that tombs in that region were simply made that way, much like cars in our day have hubcaps! The best archeological explanation that's surfaced is that people in that area and time period believed that a window was needed to allow the spirit of the dead to go free, so tombs were systematically built to accommodate that belief. Remember, this was a *borrowed* tomb!

Looking slightly to the right and a bit higher, between Elijah and Noah, you will see a dove, the symbol of the Holy Spirit, whose power raised Christ from the dead. His work has been accomplished!

Now look to the far right of the mural and up to the right corner. You will see Mount Calvary, where Jesus was crucified between two thieves three days earlier. The three crosses are still there. If you look down the outside of the mountain, you will notice that the face of a skull emerges from the mountain. That is why the hill is called Golgotha, "The Place of the Skull." That face is still there today. Looking above the crosses, you will notice a rainbow over them. This was my attempt to bring back to mind the promise of Noah when God promised that the flood was a one-time event. In the same way, the death and resurrection of Jesus was a once and for all sacrifice, never needing to be repeated! On this day Jesus paved the way to heaven. It's the day everything changed!

My model for Christ was my son, Warren. I think I may have worked him the hardest of all the others, for he played the most important part. It had to be the best of all the figures in the mural. Not only did he meet the challenge, but helped me in many other facets of the work, for which I am exceedingly grateful.

Here I would like to leave a biblical benediction with you;

May the God of peace, who through the blood of the eternal covenant brought back from the dead our Lord Jesus, that great Shepherd of the sheep, equip you with everything good for doing His will, and may He work in us what is pleasing to Him, through Jesus Christ, to whom be glory for ever and ever. Amen. Hebrews 13:20–21 ■

To view *The Resurrection Mural* online or see the available Fine Art Reproductions of the mural please go to: ***ResurrectionMural.com***

You can also visit the mural in person at the Museum of Biblical Art in Dallas, Texas.

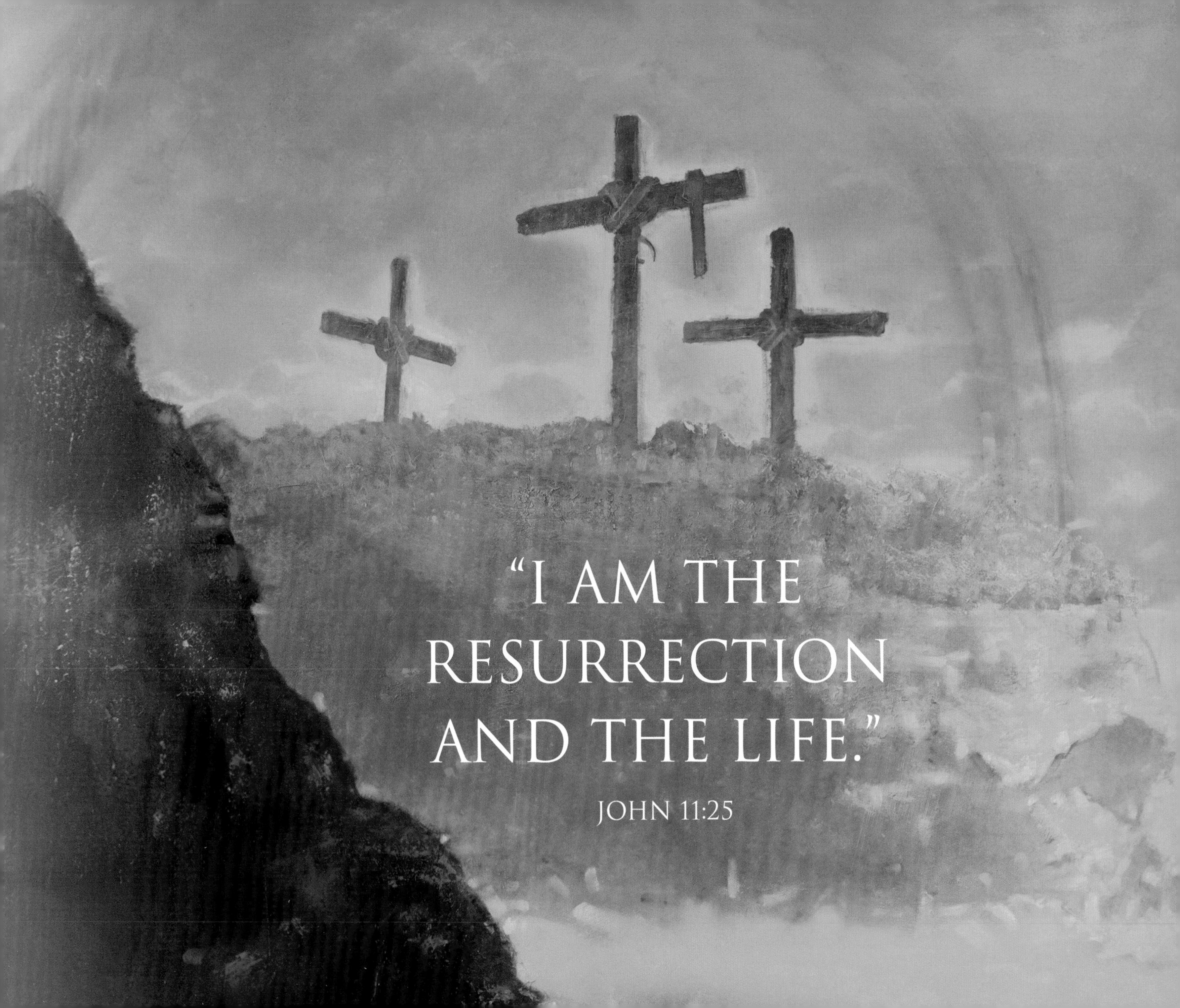
"I AM THE
RESURRECTION
AND THE LIFE."
JOHN 11:25

EPILOGUE: THE MIRROR

There is a device artists use when painting that aids them in seeing whether or not a painting is balanced and composed correctly. The artist will hold a mirror up to look at the painting so he can see it backward! This will reveal if there are some glaring mistakes that can't be seen by simply looking at it straight on.

Let's try this with the Resurrection, shall we? Working backward, let's ask ourselves some important questions and see where the facts point.

First, let's ponder the events that transpired to bring Jesus to the point of finally being placed in the tomb.

About 700 years before Jesus lived, a man by the name of Isaiah proclaimed the following message:

For to us a child is born,
to us a son is given,
and the government will be on his shoulders.
And he will be called
Wonderful Counselor, Mighty God,
Everlasting Father, Prince of Peace.
Of the increase of his government and peace
there will be no end. Isaiah 9:6–7

When the mirror is placed on Christ, there is hardly any argument that Jesus fit every bit of the criteria laid down by Isaiah. Historians, philosophers, and even other religions agree that Jesus can be described by all of what Isaiah said. If you dare, please bring evidence to the contrary. Even poems have been written about the unique, continuing, and lasting influence of Jesus Christ and how His singular life has changed the lives of untold millions.

Regarding Jesus' virgin birth, Isaiah asked the people of Israel, "Will you try the patience of my God also? Therefore the Lord himself will give you a sign: The virgin will be with child and will give birth to a son, and will call him Immanuel" (Isaiah 7:13–14). Any argument here? Does the mirror show any inconsistency? Do the facts of Jesus' birth line up exactly with that prophecy?

For those of you who are not sure, think about the ridicule that Joseph and Mary must have endured when they claimed that the conception of Jesus was without human origin. Joseph became so upset when he found out about Mary's pregnancy that he had plans to leave her (see Matthew 1). He surely didn't come up with the idea on his own. Mary, a girl of about 14 years of age, put her own reputation and life in jeopardy by such a seemingly ridiculous claim. Why (since they didn't even know what was happening to them) would they possibly risk their reputations and lives if this were not an act of God put in place to unfold the plan He gave to Isaiah 700 years earlier?

Second, let's hold the mirror up to the prophecies regarding where the Messiah would come from. Did Christ qualify? Many people of Jesus' day disputed His claim as Messiah because they thought the ancient scrolls pointed to places Jesus hadn't come from. Three of those places were Bethlehem, Egypt, and Nazareth. Taking a look in the mirror, we can see if those prophecies were indeed true.

- Jesus was born in Bethlehem of Judea. "But you, Bethlehem, in the land of Judah, are by no means least among the rulers of Judah; for out of you will come a ruler who will be the shepherd of my people Israel" (Matthew 2:6).
- Jesus was taken to Egypt by Mary and Joseph when Herod was looking to kill all the male children in order to stop any king from replacing him. When Herod died, Joseph was told in a dream, "Get up, take the child and his mother and go to the land of Israel, for those who were trying to take the child's life are dead" (Matthew 2: 20). Therefore, the prophecy of Hosea 11:1 "Out of Egypt I called my son" was fulfilled.
- Jesus was brought up in Nazareth. "Having been warned in a dream, [Joseph] withdrew to the district of Galilee, and he went and lived in a town called Nazareth. So was fulfilled what was said through the prophets: 'He will be called a Nazarene'" Matthew 2:21–23.

Next, let's put the mirror on Jesus' life. What did Jesus spend His time and energy doing? The Scripture points to three things: (1) preaching the good news of the kingdom of God (2) performing miracles, and (3) preparing for the cross. There is not one reported instance of Jesus requesting anything for Himself. (That alone makes Him unique in history, wouldn't you agree?)

Jesus' own words revealed Him as the promised Messiah. When Jesus was in the temple, He unrolled a scroll and read the following words from the book of Isaiah:

> *"The Spirit of the Lord is on me, because he has anointed me to preach good news to the poor, he has sent me to proclaim freedom for the prisoners and recovery of sight for the blind, and release the oppressed, to proclaim the year of the Lord's favor. ... Today this Scripture is fulfilled in your hearing."* Luke 4:18–19, 21

Those words describe Jesus and His ministry beautifully!

Jesus' actions confirmed He was who He said He was. The following are just a few of the many miracles that Jesus performed during His time on earth:

- He walked on water in the middle of a storm. (Mark 6:48)
- He fed thousands of people with a pittance of food—twice. (Matthew 14 and 15)
- He spoke the word and healed a centurion's servant without ever going directly to the servant. (Luke 7)
- He touched a leper and made him completely whole in front of a huge crowd. (Mark 1:40–42)
- He beat the devil in the wilderness by using the words of God. (Matthew 4)
- He calmed a storm that was so fierce, even seasoned fishermen quaked. He simply said, "Quiet! Be still!" and the very breath was instantly taken out of the storm. (Mark 4:39)
- He healed a man born blind, to the amazement of even the man's parents. (John 9)
- He forgave the sins of a paralytic and healed him. The man got up and went home. (Mark 2)
- He healed a demon-possessed man who nobody else could even tie up without his breaking the bonds. Jesus spoke the word, and the man was instantly in his right mind and fell on his knees before Jesus, recognizing who He was. (Mark 5:9–15)

These are only a fraction of the miracles recorded in Scripture, yet my imagination practically explodes when I think about all the other things Jesus did or could have done that are not even recorded. John 21:25 says:

Jesus did many other things as well. If every one of them were written down, I suppose that even the whole world would not have room for the books that would be written.

Finally, Jesus' death on the cross signaled Him as the true Messiah. Let's now turn the mirror for a final look at how Jesus took His proclamations to the ultimate degree. Again, the writing of Isaiah declares what the true Messiah would have to suffer and endure. Here are a few passages from Isaiah to consider:

See, my servant will act wisely;
he will be raised and lifted up and highly exalted.
Just as there were many who were appalled at him—
his appearance was so disfigured beyond that of any man and his form marred beyond human likeness. Isaiah 52:13–14

He was despised and rejected by men,
a man of sorrows, and familiar with suffering.
Like one from whom men hide their faces
he was despised, and we esteemed him not.
Surely he took up our infirmities
and carried our sorrows,
yet we considered him stricken by God,
smitten by him, and afflicted.
But he was pierced for our transgressions,
he was crushed for our iniquities;
the punishment that brought us peace was upon him,
and by his wounds we are healed.
We all, like sheep, have gone astray,
each of us has turned to his own way;
and the LORD has laid on him

the iniquity of us all.
He was oppressed and afflicted,
yet he did not open his mouth;
he was led like a lamb to the slaughter,
and as a sheep before her shearers is silent,
so he did not open his mouth. Isaiah 53:3–7

He was assigned a grave with the wicked,
and with the rich in his death,
though he had done no violence,
nor was any deceit in his mouth. Isaiah 53:9

Looking in the mirror, let's see how Jesus' crucifixion stacks up.

- He was "raised up" on the cross.
- He was beaten, spit on, and so mistreated by the Roman soldiers as to be unrecognizable.
- He was rejected by the Jews.
- He was familiar with suffering in the wilderness, the Garden of Gethsemane, and the cross.
- He was pierced with a spear while on the cross.
- He did not open His mouth when questioned by Pilate.
- He was led to the cross like a criminal.
- He was crucified between two thieves.

The list is endless. Still not convinced? Try one more look in the mirror. From Jesus' own mouth, He declared, *"The Son of Man is going to be betrayed into the hands of men. They will kill him, and on the third day he will be raised to life"* (Matthew 17:23). Judas was the betrayer, and the tomb only held Jesus for three days!

After He rose from the dead and walked out of His own tomb, over 500 people saw Jesus alive and whole! Not one or two, so that it could be refuted, but 500! (See 1 Corinthians 15:6.) One of His own apostles, Thomas, refused to believe until Jesus appeared to him. Jesus held out His hands for Thomas to see the nail scars and also allowed Thomas to put his hand into His side that was pierced. Thomas then came to the only conclusion that we must also come to when he declared, *"My Lord and my God!"* (John 20:28). Many have even pointed to these disciples as the best proof possible of Christ's resurrection. Before they were timid men, so afraid of even imprisonment that they ran and deserted Jesus at the first sign of trouble. But history records that each of these disciples went on to suffer and most even died for Christ rather than deny His deity. Something must have happened for these fearful men to turn into stalwart witnesses. We know what happened - they saw the risen Christ, face to face and they knew that it wasn't a hoax or a dream. Man can deny what he is told, he can ignore what he hears, but he cannot escape what he sees. What more proof do you need?

In the 2,000 years since the Resurrection, many skeptics have tried their very best to refute all the evidence, without success. In the final analysis, the words of Padre Sahib say it all:

"We have no tomb in Christianity because we have no corpse."

Hallelujah!

A SPECIAL INVITATION FROM THE AUTHOR

Within the pages of the greatest Book ever written is a road map to your future. It is a map that Jesus wrote for you so that you would not get lost on the way Home.

In order to provide you that "traveler's guide", He had to navigate some pretty grueling and amazing ground. He blazed the trails of temptation, hatred, the wrath of Satan, the abandonment of His "friends", and the cruelest death imaginable. A question needs to be asked. Why? Why would the Son of God come from the bliss of heaven to endure ridicule, give His life into the hands of hateful men, and ultimately die and be placed into a borrowed tomb?

Love is the only answer the Scriptures give. Love unlike anything humanly possible. *"For God so loved the world that he gave his one and only Son."* John 3:16

Jesus offered to take our place when we stand before God to atone for our sins. If you trust in Him and believe in Him as Lord and Savior, then you don't have any sins to account for, at least none that God will hold you responsible for. Heaven will be open to you because God was willing to lose His Son for the sake of never living without you, never having to see you go to a place He never wanted you to go.

You are the only one who can answer this invitation. It's a yes or no answer — there is no maybe.

Standing at the door is God Himself, waiting for your answer. Right now is not too early, but tomorrow may be too late. The facts are all in, and you know them well. Which way will you decide? If you decide to "take your chances" without Christ, as some have told me, then I sorrow for you. And I can only imagine how God must feel.

If, on the other hand, you recognize what's being offered to you in Jesus Christ, then tell Him now. No need to wait. Wherever you are as you are reading this, God is there, listening. Talk to Him and let Him know you accept His offer of eternal life. (That's called praying!) No matter how eloquently or clumsily you talk to God, He sees beyond the words and looks straight at the sincerity in your heart.

If I can be of help, then allow me the privilege of getting you started. You can pray the following prayer right now:

Father God, I acknowledge Jesus as my Lord and Savior. I invite Him into my heart. I know that Jesus died for me & rose again and I believe that from this moment on I am saved. Please show me Your next steps for me. Amen.

Friend, if you prayed that prayer just now, then your name was written in God's ledger in heaven. Yes, He has a book that will be opened at the end of days, and your name will be on His "invited" list!

Now, find a Bible and start reading. Find a great church and start attending. Joyfully, I look forward to the day when you and I will meet in the land where there will be no more sorrow!

ABOUT THE AUTHOR

Forty-two years ago I started out as a new illustrator, hoping to merely make a living at my gift. Little did I know that one day I would get the chance to put paint on canvas and show the world the greatest act that has ever occurred in history.

My story, however, goes back even further, to the moment I was first touched by the hand of God. My parents, both of Italian descent, lived in the inner city of Chicago, crammed in a tiny apartment with my grandmother, my mother's sister, my older brother, and a German shepherd named Jackie. When my mom became pregnant with me, there simply was no room for one more person, so an abortion was planned.

At the time, my dad was Catholic and my mom agnostic, but my grandmother was Pentecostal. I'm sure my grandmother was praying as my mom took that long walk, alone, down Grand Avenue to the doctor's office. Upon arriving at the storefront office, my mom was told the procedure would begin with a simple injection and was asked to be seated. As the syringe came within an inch of her arm, God spoke to her: *"Don't do this! I have a plan for this baby."* Obediently, my mom pushed the needle away, got up, and walked out. God came to my rescue that day. For the next 40-plus years, my mom would recount this story to me, and I would know without a doubt that God had a plan for me. *Only God.*

As a young boy, the only talent I seemed to have was drawing. However, kids from the inner city of Chicago didn't usually wind up being artists, as far as I knew. I thought that was reserved for the wealthy or privileged, of which I was neither. However, God brought a young lady into my life who believed in the talent God had given me and encouraged me to pursue my dream of becoming an artist. She would eventually become my wife. I only had one date in my entire life, and it was with Pat. That was all I needed.

I finally entered art school at the American Academy of Art in 1970. Pat bought my first easel and set of paints, and she helped put me through school. I worked as the church janitor, and she worked for an insurance company. We learned early to tithe and put God first in our lives.

One year into the Academy, my father died at work of a massive heart attack. My mom was devastated, but she knew she would see him again in heaven. Since he had no life insurance policy, I thought that would be the end of my art training. But I decided to finish out the remainder of that semester, since we had already paid for it. A week later the director of the school, a famous watercolor artist named Irving Shapiro, called me to his office. A patron had donated money to the school, and they wanted to use it to provide for me to return the next year. Stunned, I muttered, "Thank you, considering what happened to my dad." He asked, with a puzzled look, "What happened to your dad?" I told him that my father had died a week earlier. They had no idea. Again, God came to my rescue. *Only God.*

I dreamed that I would someday use the talent God had given me to serve God's kingdom. One day I shared this dream with one of my instructors, a Christian. I waited for his encouraging response, only to hear him say, "It will never happen." Crestfallen, I asked him what he meant. He explained that the Church was not interested in the Arts as it had been during the Renaissance. In his opinion, there would be no career there for anyone doing any type of Art, because the Church at large simply did not appreciate it. His advice: "Go to the world. They appreciate it!" I felt like I was unable to argue with him, and I hid my desire in my heart. But I was sure that someday God would prove my instructor wrong.

"I DREAMED THAT I WOULD SOMEDAY USE THE TALENT GOD HAD GIVEN ME TO SERVE GOD'S KINGDOM."

Two more years passed at the American Academy before I was once again called into Mr. Shapiro's office. This time he told me that, upon watching my progress over the past three years and my constantly winning the top awards the school had offered, it was time for me to leave and professionally practice all that I had learned. I was ready.

My first thought was to try to land a job at one of the most prestigious studios in the country. Art students who knew me told me I was crazy and that any chance for an artist right out of school to land that job was nearly hopeless. I went anyway. The art director conducting the interview went through my portfolio, looked at me, and asked, "Can you start on Monday?" *Only God.*

Not too long after that, I started my own business and decided to freelance. God provided for Pat and me as we married

and lived in a small garden apartment where I set up my studio. My studio was so small that when I was honored as the Official Illustrator for the Olympic Committee, I did the painting in the hallway!

As the years passed, every attempt I made to do "redeeming" work was rebuffed. Nobody was interested, so I concentrated on the major advertising agencies and Fortune 500 companies that embraced me with open arms. I accepted only work that was honorable and refused any job that did not line up with my faith in Christ. My work began to spread internationally, and jobs that I could never have imagined lined up. *Only God.*

Almost 20 years later, I felt a stirring in my soul: the time had come to follow through with my dream to devote my talent to God's work. Through a series of orchestrated events, God closed the door to secular work and slowly opened the door to "redeeming" work. Pat and I knew God was calling us to make a huge paradigm shift. But knowing God was leading, we only needed to follow — this time with two kids in tow!

One of my first commissions during this new phase was the cover of a book entitled *This Present Darkness* by Frank Peretti, an unknown author at the time. As I paced my studio floor, I asked God why He would give me a job like that. This book

contained very "dark" subject matter dealing with spiritual warfare; I wanted to do paintings that were more beautiful and less confrontational. Nevertheless, I did the cover, and God did a miracle. Not only was the book an international best seller, but God also gave me the road map He wanted me to follow, which was far better than what I had imagined! Before long, I was working with some of the finest authors, publishers, and artists in the world, and God was on the move in His kingdom. Souls were being saved, and Christians were being encouraged. I was given the privilege of helping to construct the ground floor of a Second Renaissance commissioned by God Himself. *Only God.*

God's calling on my life began in my mother's womb and continues to this day. My desire is that I may influence this generation for Christ through sight and sound, and I pray that I may be completely abandoned to God for whatever service He may need in this endeavor. My goal is that every brush stroke, every idea, and every written and spoken word be one more fragrant incense to a lost world and to the body of Christ. Please pray for me that I may continue in God's anointing until my last breath!

"ONLY GOD"

"In God's sovereignty He raises up unique people for unique tasks. I feel that He has done this with Ron DiCianni. Ron's gifted skill on canvas is but one of the ways God is using the arts to show His love. I've met few people who have both the passion and the ability to do what Ron does."

—Max Lucado

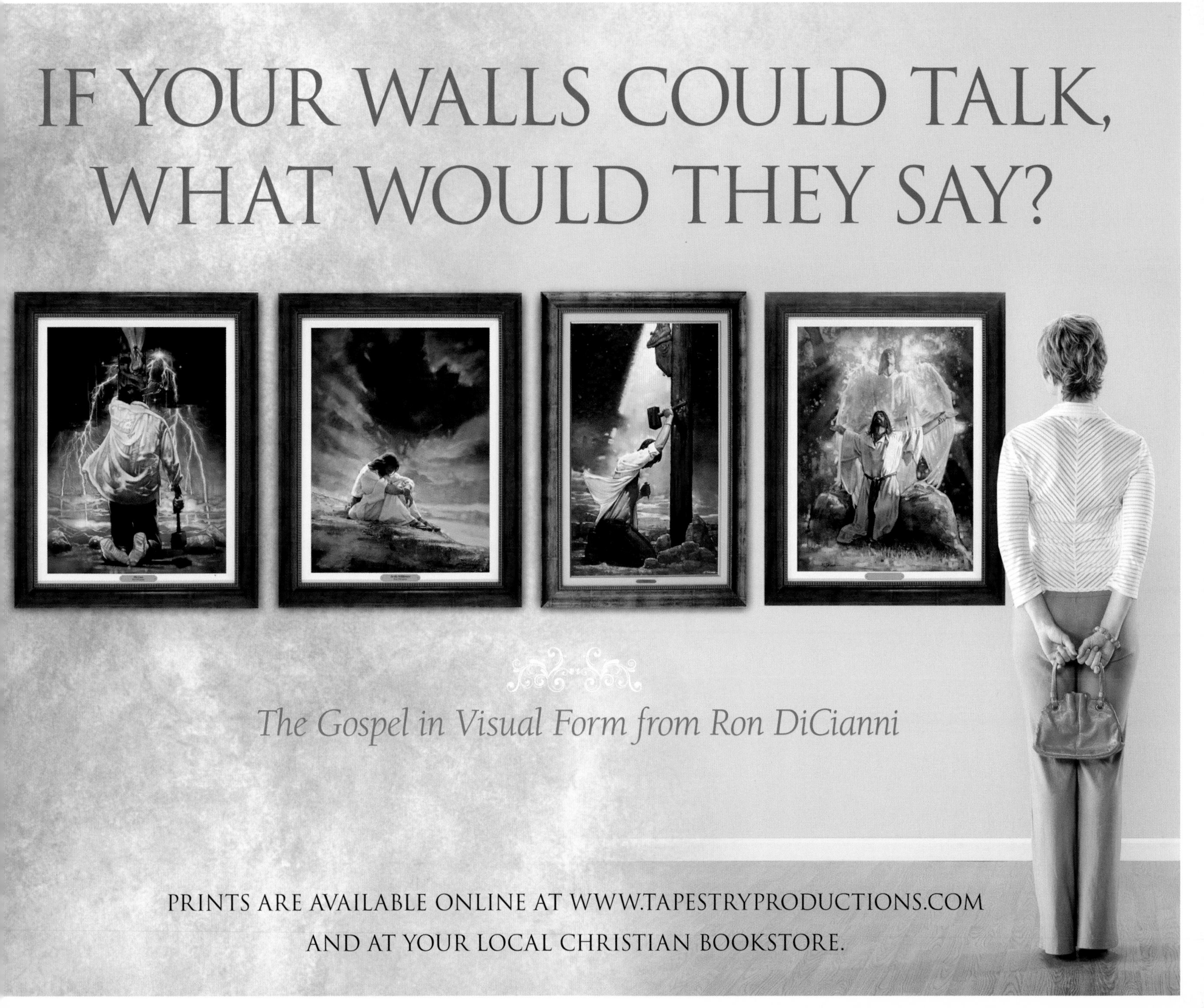
IF YOUR WALLS COULD TALK,
WHAT WOULD THEY SAY?
The Gospel in Visual Form from Ron DiCianni
PRINTS ARE AVAILABLE ONLINE AT WWW.TAPESTRYPRODUCTIONS.COM
AND AT YOUR LOCAL CHRISTIAN BOOKSTORE.